CONTENTS

Chapter 1
FROM HERODOTUS TO NAPOLEON
10

Chapter 2
SOLDIERS, PIONEERS AND ADVENTURERS
28

Chapter 3
THE SCIENTIFIC ERA
46

Chapter 4
IMMENSE TOMBS DOMINATING OTHER TOMBS
66

Chapter 5
THESES, HYPOTHESES AND REALITIES
84

DOCUMENTS
97

Chronology of the Pyramids
120

Bibliography
120

List of Illustrations
122

Index
125

Picture Credits
127

Acknowledgments
127

The Great Pyramids

JEAN-PIERRE CORTEGGIANI

DISCOVERIES®
ABRAMS, NEW YORK

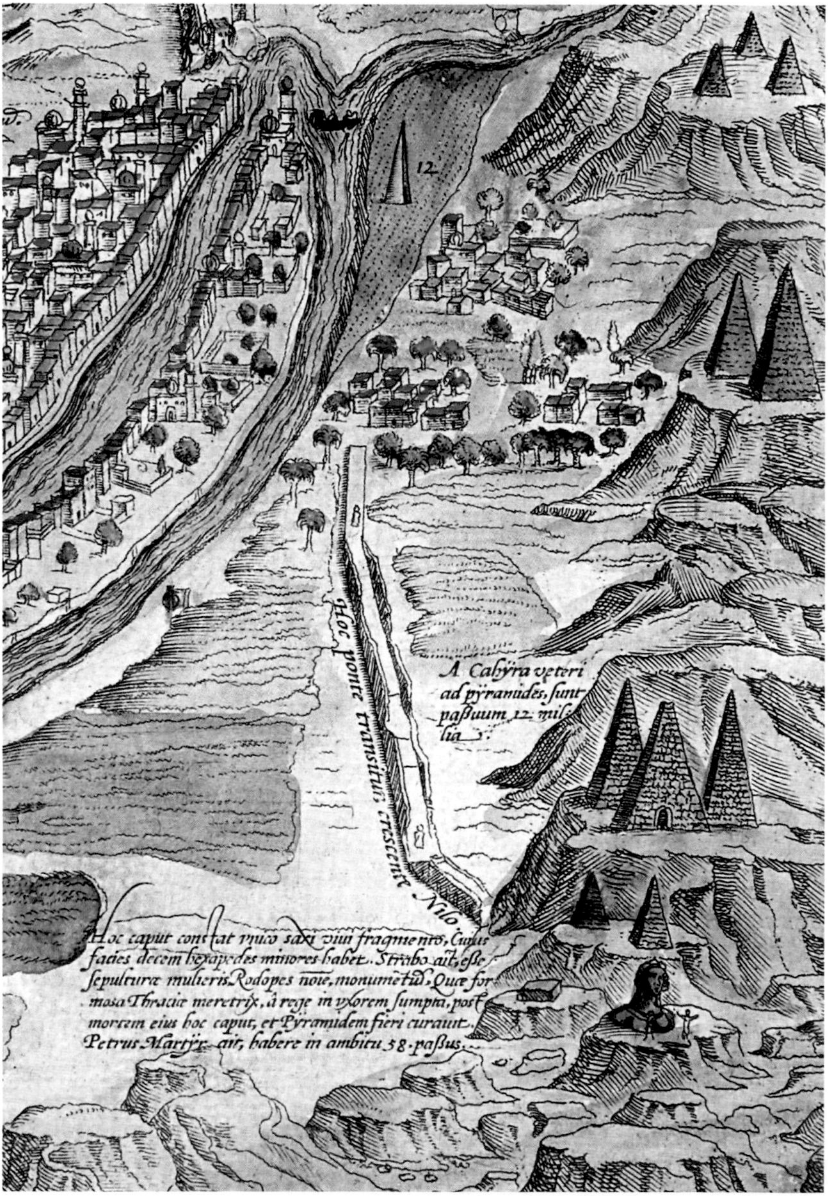

12.

Hoc ponte transitur, crescente Nilo

A Cahyra veteri
ad pyramides, sunt
paßuum 12. mil-
lia .

Hoc caput conſtat vnico saxi vni fragmento. Cuius
facies decem hexapedes minores habet. Strabo ait, eſse
sepulturæ mulieris Rodopes noïe, monumetû. Quæ for-
mosa Thraciæ meretrix, à rege in vxorem sumpta, post
mortem eius hoc caput, et Pyramidem fieri curauit.
Petrus Martyr, ait, habere in ambitu 38. paßus.

'The pyramids and temples are among the wonders known since antiquity; they have been much spoken of, and much studied as regards their function and the ancientness of their construction. [...] They have no doors, and we do not know in what manner they were built.'

Ibn Battuta, *The Travels of Ibn Battuta*, 1355–56

CHAPTER 1

FROM HERODOTUS TO NAPOLEON

Opposite: Detail of a map of Cairo, published in 1572. The illustrations in travel accounts by Egypt's first Western visitors contain a strong element of fantasy, whether they relate to the pyramids or to the Sphinx.

Right: Engravings of the Sphinx, dated 1556, 1579, 1650 and 1755.

The famous Arab geographer and traveller Ibn Battuta (1304–*c.* 1368) dictated an account of his extensive travels (spanning almost a quarter of a century) in which he notes: 'We are told that a king of Egypt [Surid] had a dream before the Flood came and was so terrified by it that he felt impelled to construct these pyramids on the western bank of the Nile. Their purpose was to serve as a repository for scientific knowledge and as tombs for the bodies of kings.' The three pyramids at Giza have always held a peculiar fascination, and in his brief commentary Ibn Battuta sums up why, pointing to an urge to see them as something more than what they are – tombs, albeit on a gigantic scale.

Left: The Greek word *pyramis* appears to refer to a pyramid-shaped wheat cake. Following Plato, for whom 'the pyramid is the solid which is the original element and seed of fire', Ammianus Marcellinus said that 'their shape received this name from the geometricians because they rise in a cone like fire'. By a process of metathesis and preceded by the definite article *pa*, the word may derive from the Egyptian word *mer* (shown here in its plural form), which appears as a small, very pointed pyramid and was used to designate the monuments themselves.

They are in fact the sepulchres of the pharaohs Khufu (Cheops), Khafre (Chephren) and Menkaure (Mycerinus), who reigned during the 4th dynasty (2575–2465 BC). They are what we picture when we think of the pyramids, the ultimate pyramids, representative of the rest but eclipsing them. However, it is worth remembering that a total of more than a hundred pyramids, of varying sizes, were constructed in Egypt as a whole, at Giza, Saqqara, Meidum, Dahshur and Abu Roash, among other places.

When it comes to the size and scale of its monuments, ancient Egypt does not hold a monopoly: the tomb of China's first emperor, buried with his Terracotta Army, is equal to the pyramids in this respect, and yet the mausoleum of Qin Shi Huang (260–210 BC) has exerted

Below, from left to right: The pyramids of Menkaure, Khafre (with the remains of its casing at the top) and Khufu.

far less impact on the human imagination. The same is true of the Great Wall of China, despite its vast span (over 6,000 km). The fact is that no other civilization has ever created a monument that excited as much amazement, admiration and speculation as these vast stone edifices, which were already two thousand years old when the Greeks gave them the name *pyramis* – a word whose etymology remains uncertain.

Tombs for Eternity

As if the mere fact of leaving such monuments to posterity was enough in itself, the ancient Egyptians had little to say on the subject of the pyramids. The small brick pyramids built over the private tombs of the New Kingdom are widely depicted, but there are very few pictures of the great pyramids. The oldest known depiction is by the scribe Montuher and was found on a commemorative stela near the Sphinx, which had become a site of pilgrimage by the time of Ramesses II (1290–1224 BC).

We know that a number of literate scribes of the 18th and 19th dynasties (*c.* 1550–1187 BC) came to Saqqara to see the oldest pyramid, the Step Pyramid of Djoser, because these 'tourists' left graffiti in the vicinity of the

Below: On the stela dedicated by the scribe Montuher to the god Horemakhet ('Horus at the Horizon'), only the two largest pyramids are represented behind the image of the Great Sphinx. The colossus was known as Horemakhet and worshipped as an entirely separate divinity from the beginning of the 18th dynasty.

monument expressing their admiration. We can only speculate as to whether such visitors also travelled to Giza in order to admire the largest of all the pyramids while these were still intact. It is possible, since the first travellers to see them with their casing still in place mention inscriptions, but if such glowing commentaries existed they have since disappeared along with the layer of fine limestone that once covered the pyramids.

From the outset the pyramid was evidently synonymous with the notion of eternity. This much is clear from the Pyramid Texts, the funerary texts covering the walls of royal tombs from the end of the 5th dynasty (2465–2323 BC): in numerous instances all the gods are invoked in order to ensure that the royal sepulchre might be 'in a perfect state and endure for eternity'. A literary text, the *Chester Beatty IV* papyrus, conserved in the British Museum, conveys this notion of eternity through a very different context, praising the scribe – or, in other words, the writer – and stating in essence that a book confers eternal life on its author more effectively than a pyramid can.

The First Witness

It is to the 'Father of History' that we owe the first description of the pyramids: Herodotus, who visited Egypt towards the middle of the 5th century BC and devoted a few pages in the second book of his *History* (*Euterpe*) to the prestigious monuments at Giza and to the men who constructed them. There are significant errors in Herodotus's account, but for almost twenty-five centuries this was *the* text on the pyramids and their so-called 'mysteries', universally referred to, quoted and interpreted, albeit selectively – as a means of supporting its readers' assumptions.

The main part of Herodotus's account deals with the construction of the Great Pyramid, although a close reading reveals that what he is in fact describing is the final stage, during which the monument was encased in fine white Turah limestone with 'the aid of machines constructed of short pieces of wood'. There is nothing to indicate (though it has often been affirmed) that these 'machines' were used to construct the internal steps, and we may assume that if Herodotus failed to allude to the use of 'ramps', this was because he took the causeway linking the upper and lower temples for the route along which the stones were dragged, with the result that this aspect of the construction process seemed to him self-evident.

The Only 'Wonder' to Have Survived the Passage of Time

In an Arabic proverb time itself is said to fear the pyramids, and it has often been stressed that of all the Seven Wonders of the Ancient World the pyramids are

Opposite: Pyramid Texts are engraved on the walls of the funerary apartments of some ten pyramids at Saqqara. Their earliest appearance is in Unas's burial chamber and antechamber. Unas (2356–2323 BC) was the last king of the 5th dynasty, but the elaboration of this substantial funerary corpus must in fact have spanned several centuries. Given its importance, it would be very surprising if it had not been available to the king's predecessors and, in particular, the great rulers of the 4th dynasty such as Khufu, Khafre and Menkaure, probably in the form of a roll of papyrus bearing the formulas of what appears to have been known as the 'Book of the God' (Thoth being the god in question).

Left: Attempts to illustrate the construction of Khufu's pyramid were based on the description by Herodotus. This drawing depicts the 'machines' – essentially a system of levers – supposedly used to raise the stone blocks (represented as much longer than they are in reality) from one course to the next.

the only ones to have survived to the present day. This is clearly true, but we need to be more specific as there are various different lists that itemize the architectural masterpieces of antiquity, and not all of them consider the three pyramids together as an exceptional achievement of human genius.

In the 2nd century BC, the Greek poet Antipater of Sidon mentioned 'the huge labour of the high pyramids' in an epigram, which is the first known reference to the Seven Wonders of the Ancient World. The Greek historian Diodorus Siculus, writing in the 1st century BC, stated that Khufu 'built the greatest of the three pyramids, which were accounted amongst the seven wonders of the world'. A later list, from around the 4th or 5th century AD and widely attributed to Philo of Byzantium (an obscure engineer not to be confused with the Alexandrian scholar of the same name living in the 3rd century BC), also speaks of the 'Pyramids of Memphis'. By contrast, the Roman geographer Strabo, in the 1st century AD, wrote that 'two out of the three are counted among the Seven Wonders of the World'.

Herodotus's Successors

Four centuries after Herodotus came several accounts of the pyramids, written by classical authors who were virtually contemporaries of one another and entirely in agreement over the funerary nature of these vast monuments. In the first volume of his *Historical Library* (Book I, LXIII–LXIV), Diodorus Siculus asserts that the stones, which were 'without the least decay', were set in place by 'making mounts of earth; cranes and other engines being not known at that time'. Substantiating thereby the use of ramps, he notes how surprising it is to 'see such a foundation so imprudently laid, as it seems to be, in a sandy place, where there is not the least sign of any earth cast up, nor marks where any stone was cut and polished; so that the whole pile seems to be reared all at once, and fixed in the midst of heaps of sand by some god, and not built by degrees by the hands of men.' Later he assures us that none of the kings who built them to serve as their tombs was actually buried in the pyramids, thereby adding fuel to the more absurd theories.

Above: Engraving by the 16th-century Dutch artist Maerten Van Heemskerck, one of a series devoted to the Seven Wonders of the World.

PIRAMIDES ÆGYPTI

Strabo refers to the pyramids briefly in his *Geography* (Book XVII), providing an important insight into the archaeological history of the Great Pyramid. From this work, we gather that the location of the entrance was known in Strabo's day. He tells us that it was closed by 'a movable stone which, once it was removed, gave access to a sloping gallery leading down to the tomb'. Strabo, along with a number of other writers, attributes the

Van Heemskerck had never been to Egypt and his vision of the pyramids derives from his imagination, like the images of the Lighthouse of Alexandria, the Hanging Gardens of Babylon and the other lost Wonders.

pyramid of Menkaure to a courtesan by the name
of Rhodopis. In this ancient Egyptian variant of the
Cinderella story, a sandal (probably made of papyrus)
takes the place of the glass slipper.

Finally, Pliny the Elder, writing in the 1st century AD
(*The Natural History*, Book XXXVI), described the
pyramids as no more than 'idle and frivolous pieces of
ostentation of their resources, on the part of the monarchs
of that country'. He says that his predecessors 'disagreed as
to the persons by whom they were constructed; accident
having [...] consigned to oblivion the names of those
who erected such stupendous memorials of their vanity'.
The principal question that we must ask ourselves, he says,
is how such vast blocks of stone could have been raised
to such a great height.

A Centuries-long Eclipse

In the centuries that followed, references to the pyramids
were few and far between. The *Augustan History*, a late
Roman collection of biographies of the
Roman emperors of the 2nd and 3rd
centuries, tells us that in 200 Septimius
Severus 'paid a thorough visit to
Memphis, the statue of Memnon,
the Pyramids and the Labyrinth',
and between 388 and 391 the Greek
Ammianus Marcellinus, the last of
the great Roman historians, described
the pyramids as 'towers rising above
anything the hand of man can create',
reminding us that these same
monuments had been 'promoted to
the rank of the Seven Wonders' (Book
XXII). With the exception of such
rare allusions, however, the pyramids
remained shrouded in almost total
silence for the remainder of the
millennium.

They continued to attract visitors,
but these were Christians making the
pilgrimage to the Holy Land, following
the lead of Constantine the Great's

B elow: Constructed
in Rome at the end
of the 1st century BC
and later inserted into
the Aurelian Wall, near
the San Paolo gate, Caius
Cestius's slender pyramid
clearly served as a model
for artists illustrating the
Giza pyramids without
first-hand knowledge of
them. In terms of shape
it resembles much more
closely the 4th-century
BC pyramids at Meroë
in Sudan.

mother, the Empress Helena, who in a sense launched the fashion for such visits when she travelled to Jerusalem in 326. These visitors were indifferent to anything foreign to their faith (whose triumph was assured by the edicts of the Roman Emperor Theodosius I in 392, declaring Christianity as the only legitimate state religion) and devoted their efforts not to the appreciation of ancient monuments but to following in the footsteps of Christ and, in the case of Egypt, retracing the routes taken by the slaves during the Exodus and later by the Holy Family. From *Egeria's Travels*, a letter by a noble Galician lady who made a pilgrimage to the Holy Land between 381 and 384, it is clear that seeing Sinai, the 'mountain of God', was what mattered, not the pyramids, the 'mountains of Pharaoh'. The biblical references were paramount and, as Rufinus of Aquileia tells us, the pyramids were simply 'Joseph's granaries'.

Arab Travellers and Geographers

The most important work by erudite Egyptian historian al-Maqrizi (1364–1442), translated into French by Urbain Bouriant as *Description topographique et historique de l'Egypte*, devotes a chapter to the pyramids. From the first

Above: This famous 13th-century mosaic, one of a number of biblical scenes in St Mark's Basilica in Venice, shows the pyramids as the granaries (complete with openings for the sheaves) in which, after interpreting Pharaoh's dream, Joseph 'stored up grain in great abundance, like the sand of the sea' in anticipation of the seven years of famine (Genesis, 41:49). The notion of the pyramids as Joseph's granaries had been widely accepted throughout the Christian world for almost a thousand years even though, in the 9th century, a patriarch of Antioch affirmed that they were royal tombs, 'oblique and solid and not hollow and empty'.

half of the 15th century, it forms a (somewhat repetitive) compilation of all the texts of the principal Arab writers before him. Alongside sensible and historically informative observations are legends and accounts full of the fantasy that was characteristic of Arabic literature at the time, with a wealth of titles such as *The Summary of Wonders* and the *Book of Buried Pearls and of the Precious Mystery, Giving Indications Regarding the Hiding Places of Finds and Treasures*.

In his *Account of Egypt*, Abd al-Latif (1162–1231), an 'Arab doctor from Baghdad', expresses his admiration at the sight of the pyramids of Khufu and Khafre, 'compared' by the poets 'to two immense breasts rising up from the bosom of Egypt'. He enthuses over the size of the blocks and 'the extreme precision with which these stones have been bonded and arranged one on top of the other' and notes correctly (though in fact he is referring only to the source of the casing stones): 'Facing the pyramids, on the eastern bank of the Nile, a large number of excavations are visible. These excavations are vast and very deep, and they are interconnected. [...] These are quite clearly the quarries from which the stones for building the pyramids were extracted.'

The Andalusian Abu Hamid al-Gharnati, writing a short time earlier, stressed the 'artfulness' with which the stones of the Great Pyramid had been fitted, cut and levelled, an artfulness that 'no skilled carpenter would be able to match, making a small wooden box based on the same design', and he also spoke of a 'passage through which water flows down on to the mill'. In an account

Below and opposite: The two images of the pyramids, taken from a manuscript by Abu Hamid al-Gharnati (also known as al-Qaysi and al-Andalusi), are among the very few to be found in Arabic writings. A native of Granada, al-Gharnati died in Damascus in *c.* 1169–70, leaving behind a 'collection of wonders' and an account of his travels, two works that describe the pyramids 'facing Misr al-Fustat' (Cairo) in almost identical terms.

worthy of *One Thousand and One Nights*, he describes the occasion when Caliph Abdallah al-Mamun (786–833), son of Haroun al-Rashid, broke into Khufu's pyramid. The body discovered inside 'a statue of a man carved in green stone' (in other words, an anthropoid statue of necessarily late date), with its 'coat of gold mail, decorated with all manner of precious stones', its 'priceless sword scabbard' and the 'ruby the size of a hen's egg' on its head, was certainly not the body of Khufu, though the spectre of Ali Baba seems to be hovering over the scene!

In the middle of the 10th century, the historian Ali al-Masudi recounted how al-Mamun, unable to fulfil his wish of destroying a pyramid, contented himself with giving the order to break into the largest. He told how blacksmiths used a combination of levers and fire and vinegar to achieve this, and how they found 'a green basin at the bottom of the hole' containing a thousand dinars, the exact amount of gold it had cost to break into the pyramid. The caliph was consequently 'filled with astonishment on seeing that the ancients had known the precise sum that would be spent and the precise spot the bowl of dinars would be found'.

We also learn that the casing of the pyramids was used by the Sultan Saladin in the 12th century to build 'the Citadel of the Mountain, the perimeter wall at Cairo and Masr, and the Giza bridges', and it was his son Othman who, following poor advice, 'disfigured' the

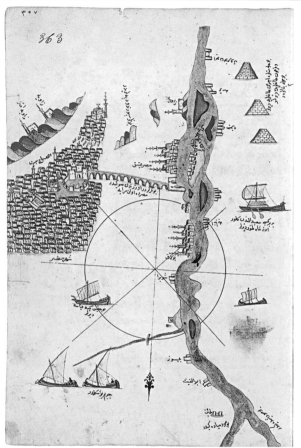

Left: The 16th-century portolano, known as the *Book of Navigation*, by the Turkish admiral Piri Reis depicted more of Egypt than just its Mediterranean coastline. This map (with north at the bottom) shows the Nile on a level with Cairo, before it divides into two branches, at the apex of the Delta. On the right bank, massed at the foot of the Mokattam Hills, the Ottoman capital is connected to the river by Saladin's aqueduct, which supplied it with water. On the left bank, three pyramids, with their heads lopped off and their casing removed, seem to have been positioned there without any reference to geographical precision – perhaps as a reminder that they had served in part as quarries, relinquishing their fine limestone casing since Fatimid times in order to build the city's perimeter walls. Excavations at Djedefre's pyramid at Abu Roash have shown in fact that Khafre's tomb was being robbed of its stone as early as the Roman era and, as English Egyptologist Flinders Petrie (1853–1942) tells us, such exploitation was still taking place at the end of the 19th century.

north face of the Pyramid of Menkaure while making a vain attempt to break into it. One of the reasons that al-Maqrizi's compilation is so interesting is that it recounts in great detail the various Arab legends linked with the pyramids and in particular that of King Surid, in *The Summary of Wonders*, according to which the gigantic monuments at Giza served as receptacles for hieratic knowledge and wisdom. In some quarters they were identified as the tombs of the Greek gods Hermes and Agathodaemon – certain to delight lovers of the esoteric.

Western Travellers and Pilgrims

At the top of the Great Pyramid is a platform 10 m² which cannot be seen from the ground. The stones up there are covered with graffiti left by visitors. Among them, the isolated date 1355 indicates that Western travellers were climbing the pyramid (whose casing had by then disappeared) from as early as the mid-14th century, if not before.

After the last crusade less than a century earlier, Western travellers, most of whom were pilgrims travelling to the Holy Land, began to take note of the country they passed through on their way to or from their destination, and the pyramids became an obligatory stopping point. More than two hundred and fifty published travel accounts have been recorded for the period between the 15th and the beginning of the 18th centuries. There is a great deal of repetition and a number of authors had almost certainly not seen the monuments for themselves, drawing their inspiration from the works of contemporaries and classical authors, and yet none of these texts is without interest. One of the most interesting writers is Sir John Mandeville, whose book of travels is dated 1356. Despite remarks (in many respects accurate) regarding 'Joseph's granaries', which he tells us may be 'sepulchres belonging to great lords of the past', the Great Pyramid appears in his work as a tower, perhaps simply because Ammianus Marcellinus described it in this way – as the Czech nobleman Krystof Harant was to do more than two centuries later.

One of the earliest accounts, written by the Fleming Joos Van Ghistele, who served under Charles the Bold, Duke of Burgundy, prior to his arrival in Egypt in 1482, tells a curious story relating to the Sphinx. He recounts how a man came to consult the 'idol', which 'was in the

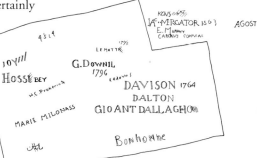

Below: Over the centuries, a lot of graffiti has been engraved on the stones of the Great Pyramid (mainly round the entrance and at the top) – the names and initials of pilgrims, merchants, missionaries, scholars, soldiers and famous travellers, who were able to climb the monument because its smooth limestone casing had disappeared. The stone that is located to the right of the main entrance bears, one above the other, the 'signatures' left, in 1563 and 1764 respectively, by Gerardus Mercator, the renowned Flemish cartographer, and Nathaniel Davison, the British diplomat who discovered the access to the first 'stress-relieving chamber' (Davison's Chamber). Higher up there are the words 'Their indestructible mass has exhausted time', a line from a poem by the Abbé Delille (1738–1813), referring to Rome's monuments.

habit of speaking in the days when idolatry was common practice', and asked the Sphinx 'what would happen to him, and the head replied that he would become king and lord of Egypt'. The story has too many points in common with that of Thutmose IV, engraved on the famous Dream Stela, for us to disregard the probable link with an oral tradition that would appear to have lasted for nearly three thousand years (despite the lack of other evidence).

A number of writers take up the idea that the builder of the Great Pyramid was the 'pharaoh who drowned himself in the Red Sea'. This is what André Thevet tells us in his *Cosmographie de Levant* (1554), although he also mentions Khufu. He describes it as 'improbable' that the pyramids were 'supports for the Pharaoh's granaries', because, he tells us, he saw in one of them 'a huge marble stone, fashioned in the shape of a tomb'. Illustrating his text is a picture of a curly-haired head, the earliest 'modern' image of the sphinx, along with a strangely pointed pyramid which looks much more like the funerary monument of Caius Cestius in Rome than Khufu's tomb. The fact that for a long time people who had actually seen the pyramids for themselves represented them in this fashion – in a way curiously similar to the Egyptian hieroglyphic sign and the pyramids of Sudan – suggests that these writers were variously influenced by the Roman tomb, to which Robert Huntington (in 1695) and a number of others alluded.

The Journey to Egypt: A Wealth of Accounts

Looking at the various written accounts, we can piece together details of the exploration into the internal structure of the Great Pyramid, which was the only one to remain accessible right up to the beginning of the 19th century. For some it appears to have been their life's adventure, particularly those who attempted to enter the 'well' connecting the Grand Gallery with the Descending Passage towards the first, unfinished Subterranean Chamber.

The pyramids were beginning to lose a little of their mystery. In 1646, the Englishman John Greaves published his *Pyramidographia, or a Description of the Pyramids in Ægypt*, which may be regarded as the first scientific evaluation of the famous monuments. A few years later, in 1678, one Ellis Veryard describes them as no more than 'prodigious Heaps of wrought Stone', although he also saw them as hieroglyphs of the immortality of the soul. Travel accounts referring to the pyramids, some at length, others less so, followed in quick succession during the second half of the 17th century and throughout the 18th century.

B elow: Writers who had not visited Egypt were quite prepared to borrow from those who had, and the same imaginary views of the pyramids, sometimes only bar a few details, are to be found in a number of different works. This engraving is a case in point. Taken from the *Description de l'Afrique* published in 1686 by the Dutchman Olfert Dapper, the illustration – in which the Sphinx appears twice in a landscape littered with pyramids – was later re-used by the engraver Pieter Van der Aa in his *Galerie agréable du monde* (1729).

We should mention for the record (though the list is far from exhaustive) Jean de Thévenot's *The Travels of Monsieur de Thévenot into the Levant* (first published in French in 1664), Father Vansleb's *Nouvelle relation en forme de journal d'un voyage fait en Égypte* (1677), *Voyage du Sieur Paul Lucas au Levant* (1705), Benoît de Maillet's *Description de l'Égypte* (1735), including the first published cross-section of the Great Pyramid, *A Description of the East, and Some Other Countries* by the Englishman Richard Pococke (1743–45), Dane Frederick Norden's *Travels* (1755), and Claude Louis Fourmont's *Description historique et géographique des plaines d'Héliopolis et de Memphis* (1755).

Two books steeped in the philosophy of the Enlightenment were published on the eve of the French Revolution – Claude Savary's *Letters on Egypt* (1786) and Constantin François Volney's *Travels through Syria and Egypt* (1787) – and exerted a powerful influence in intellectual and political circles. These two authors did more than simply describe the pyramids and other monuments: they conveyed their personal reflections on the country and, in almost identical terms, suggested conquering Egypt. For Savary, 'in the hands of a nation friendly to the arts, this beautiful country would become the centre of world commerce. It would be the bridge that would reunite Europe and Asia….' Volney said much the same thing: 'Were Egypt possessed by a nation friendly to the fine arts, discoveries might be made there, which would make us better acquainted with antiquity than any thing the rest of the world can afford us….' It is unsurprising to learn that his account was used virtually as a travel guide by Napoleon.

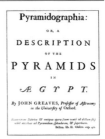

Above and below: Many of the travelogues published between the middle of the 15th and the end of the 18th centuries are inspired by other accounts or quote extensively from classical authors, and yet each of them has its own contribution to make to Giza's great royal tombs.

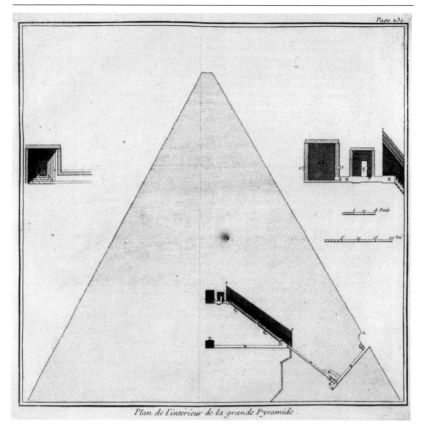

Page 230.

Plan de l'intérieur de la grande Pyramide.

Above: Although its proportions are wrong, this section of the Great Pyramid by Benoît de Maillet (1735) shows what was known at the time regarding its internal structure, including the 'granite plugs' at the juncture of the Descending and Ascending passages. The Subterranean Chamber and relieving chambers had yet to be discovered.

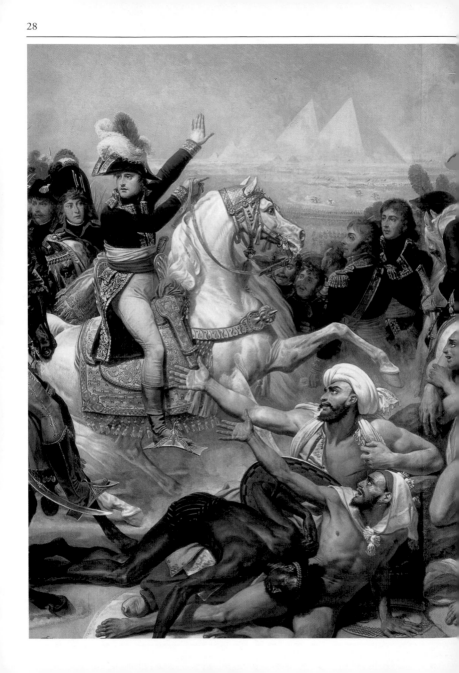

In the first half of the 19th century, Egypt attracted a series of foreign expeditions, from Napoleon's famous Egyptian expedition, which ended in the autumn of 1801, to the Prussian expedition led by Karl Richard Lepsius (1810–84) between 1842 and 1845. Their primary aim was to excavate and, above all, to study the pharaonic monuments – in particular the Giza pyramids – in what was to prove an increasingly scientific spirit.

CHAPTER 2

SOLDIERS, PIONEERS AND ADVENTURERS

Despite his victories at the Battle of the Pyramids in 1798 (opposite) and Aboukir in 1799, Napoleon's Egyptian campaign may not have been the military success he had anticipated. However, the expedition was exceptionally fruitful from a scientific point of view, as demonstrated by the thousands of pages and hundreds of plates in the *Description de l'Égypte* (right), published from 1809.

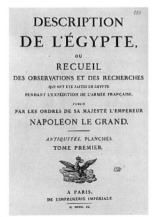

DESCRIPTION
DE L'ÉGYPTE,
OU
RECUEIL
DES OBSERVATIONS ET DES RECHERCHES
QUI ONT ÉTÉ FAITES EN ÉGYPTE
PENDANT L'EXPÉDITION DE L'ARMÉE FRANÇAISE,
PUBLIÉ
PAR LES ORDRES DE SA MAJESTÉ L'EMPEREUR
NAPOLÉON LE GRAND.

ANTIQUITÉS. PLANCHES.
TOME PREMIER.

A PARIS,
DE L'IMPRIMERIE IMPÉRIALE.
M. DCCC. IX.

'Glorious feats of arms allied to the discovery of works of art'

This was how Napoleon Bonaparte described the Egyptian expedition. He and his troops set sail with a veritable battalion of scientific experts – 'a third of the Institut' in Napoleon's words – and in this respect surpassed even the efforts of Alexander the Great in the 4th century BC. The realization, albeit incomplete, of Napoleon's Oriental dream marked the beginning of Egypt's rediscovery and the rediscovery of its ancient civilization. The two editions of the monumental *Description de l'Égypte* are the fruits of a little more than three years' worth of work in which exhaustive records, measurements and descriptions of the country's principal features were compiled.

The three pyramids were to be for ever linked with Napoleon's exploits by the latter's famous words of encouragement to his men on the eve of battle – a battle which, though it was known as the Battle of the Pyramids, was not in fact fought in their vicinity. A mere three weeks had elapsed since the army disembarked at Alexandria on 1 July 1798, but it was not until the beginning of 1801 that the engineer Jean-Marie Coutelle and the architect Jean-Baptiste Lepère 'ensconced themselves in the desert' and began a detailed study of the monuments. By this time Napoleon had left Egypt to pursue his imperial fortunes elsewhere; General Kléber had been assassinated and it was his successor Jacques-François de Menou who had appointed Coutelle and Lepère to the task of directing excavations

A bove: This detail from a painted ceiling in the Louvre brings together an odd assortment of objects, including military uniforms, a stela and a canopic jar. Napoleon is in the background. The composition is reminiscent of the peculiar nature of this expedition, which was to become more of a scientific than a military exercise.

O pposite, top left: The cross-section of the Antechamber (1), between the Grand Gallery (2) and the King's Chamber (3), shows the precision of Coutelle's surveys.

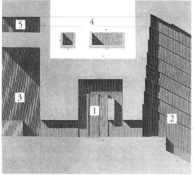

Left: At the top of the Grand Gallery, a figure is seen climbing into the narrow passage (4) that gives access to the first relieving chamber (5).

Below: The Grand Gallery seen from the bottom, at the upper entrance to the 'well'.

and research at Giza, Saqqara and the Memphis site.

In 'Observations on the Pyramids of Gyzeh and on the Surrounding Monuments and Constructions', later published in the *Description de l'Égypte*, Coutelle recalls 'the programme of works' and the conditions under which these were executed: 'A hundred men on guard duty, under my command, protected us against the risk of Arab incursions; a hundred and fifty Turkish workers, together with a section of the troops, were engaged in searching for the base of the Great Pyramid and demolishing one of the smallest ones, opening up the well of the Great Pyramid, uncovering the Sphinx and excavating the tombs. While the first works were being carried out, we set about locating and measuring the entrance to the Great Pyramid, along with the galleries and chambers which (though they had been described by earlier travellers) also formed part of our research.'

Coutelle records the principal measurements for the various sections of the Great Pyramid – or at any rate those that were known at the time – and describes its internal layout, devoting particular attention to the 'portcullis Antechamber' (and correctly analysing the mechanism for sealing it), the 'vacant space above the burial chamber', in other words, the first 'stress-relieving chamber', which he was probably the first to define as such, and the 'well', which he had started to clear in the hope of 'discovering the motive that lay behind such a laborious piece of construction'.

As others had done before him, in particular the engineer and archaeologist Edmé François Jomard using physical measurements, and the astronomer N. A. Nouet through trigonometric calculations, Coutelle and his alter ego attempted to record the precise dimensions of the monument, calculating the angles of the northern side in order to establish those of the base and using an instrument developed by Lepère to measure the height 'of all the steps of the Great Pyramid, starting from the top'. They estimated the length of the base to be 2.4 metres longer than the figure generally accepted today (230.34 metres) and counted 203 courses, although only 201 have in fact been preserved. However, the figure they arrived at for the height is only fifteen centimetres less than the 138.745 metres measured by Georges Goyon in the 1940s.

The plan of the site and the cross-section of the Great Pyramid contain a few inaccuracies (there are not six small pyramids to the south of Khufu's and the King's Chamber is offset south from the centre axis), but the drawings and surveys produced by Coutelle and Lepère are nevertheless a remarkable achievement. By contrast, the lengthy description of the monuments provided by Jomard contains observations of a highly unscientific nature and served to fuel much wild speculation. In the eyes of the future imperial commissioner responsible for the publication of the *Description de l'Égypte*, who was only twenty-four at the time, 'everything that relates to the monument's construction and the manner of its arrangement [...] is mysterious'. 'It is no doubt reasonable to suppose that mysteries were celebrated in such an edifice,' he writes, 'or that initiations may have been practised in the lower chambers, and cult ceremonies generally, religious rites', and he goes so far as to say: 'In these monuments, and particularly in the first pyramid, the

B elow: Charles Balzac's *View of the Pyramids and the Sphinx at Sunset*, painted for the *Description de l'Égypte*, is a 'panorama' in the real sense of the term, providing an uninterrupted view of the site. The figures on top of the Sphinx's head are taking measurements.

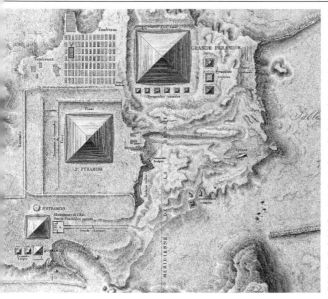

Left: The maps and sections that were produced during the French occupation of Egypt are perhaps even more impressive than the surveys of the monuments, particularly when we think how rapidly the work was carried out: in the space of just three years 1:100,000-scale maps were produced for the whole of Egypt and Palestine. This topographical map of the 'Pyramids of Memphis', established for a vast, as yet unexcavated area and one still largely covered with sand at the time, shows not only the three pyramids themselves but almost all the elements of each pyramid complex, including Khafre's and Menkaure's mortuary temples, Menkaure's 'grand causeway', the queens' pyramids, the Sphinx, outer walls, and mastabas in the Western Cemetery.

funerary purpose is by no means the principal object, and it has not even been proved that any king was ever placed there after his death.'

A Genoese Sailor and the Paduan Strongman

In the years following the departure of Napoleon's troops, the search for antiquities rapidly gathered pace, fuelled by the efforts of consuls such as Henry Salt, Bernardino Drovetti and Giovanni Anastasi, who had more of the collector about them than the diplomat.

Khufu's burial chamber (opposite) and the Grand Gallery (left), seen from the juncture with the Ascending Passage, form part of a series of engravings by the Italian Luigi Mayer, published in his *Views in Egypt* (1804). In addition to the great collaborative works such as the *Description de l'Égypte* (1809–28), the *Denkmaeler aus Aegypten und Aethiopien* (1849–59), produced by the Prussian expedition, and the *Monuments de l'Égypte et de la Nubie* (1835–45) and *Monumenti dell'Egitto e della Nubia* (1832–44), published independently by the renowned Egyptologists Jean-François Champollion and Ippolito Rosellini following their joint expedition, the 19th century also saw the publication of a number of works by individual authors, artists and Egyptologists. Vivant Denon, one of the most eminent members of Napoleon's expedition, published his *Travels in Upper and Lower Egypt* in 1802, and between 1858 and 1877 the civil engineer and hydrographer Prisse d'Avennes, one of the pioneers of Egyptology, published his *Atlas of Egyptian Art*.

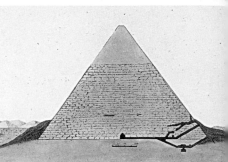

New discoveries were made in the pyramids of Khufu and Khafre by two Italians who were not members of any artistic or scientific commission but were being privately financed to carry out excavations. Giovanni Battista Caviglia (1770–1845), a merchant seaman from Genoa, was attempting a partial excavation of the Sphinx and also focusing his efforts on the Great Pyramid. In 1817, he started clearing the well – a task that Coutelle and Lepère had been obliged to interrupt on military orders – but was unable to reach the bottom of the shaft. He proceeded to construct several 'saps', which were rapidly abandoned, in particular in the 'Queen's Chamber'. He then decided to clear the Descending Passage, which was still filled with debris up to the level of the granite plugs, and in this way reached the unfinished chamber hollowed out from the rock at a depth of 30 metres 'beneath the centre of the pyramid'. He had previously located the juncture of the well with the Descending Passage, which had enabled him to finish emptying the bottom of the well and re-establish the air circulation with the upper galleries.

These operations were witnessed by Giovanni Battista Belzoni (1778–1823), who was to give an account of them in the first volume of his *Travels in Egypt and Nubia*, published in 1821. Belzoni had been a circus strongman in London and had gone to Egypt in the hope of selling a hydraulic machine, which he offered in vain to the viceroy Muhammad Ali. It is to this colourful character that we

*B*elow: This engraving of Belzoni shows him dressed in Oriental garb, following a fashion that was current among European visitors to Egypt and also adopted by Champollion.

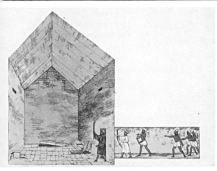

owe the discovery of the entrance to Khafre's pyramid, which had simply been concealed by the mass of rubble that had accumulated when medieval quarrymen removed the fine limestone casing. When, on 2 March 1818, a year after discovering the vast tomb of Seti I in the Valley of the Kings, Belzoni broke into Khafre's burial chamber, he discovered an 'Arabic inscription' proving to him that, though he may have been the first European to enter, he had been preceded 'by a number of Egypt's Mohammedan rulers' in the last third of the 14th century. He may have been trying to erase that memory when he wrote his name and the date of his discovery in huge letters along one wall of the chamber.

Belzoni set about clearing Khafre's burial chamber, which, despite its double entrance, was a great deal simpler than Khufu's. Drawing parallels between the two royal tombs, he expressed his surprise that not a single hieroglyph was to be found either outside or inside these gigantic monuments, concluding that the absence of hieroglyphs proved nothing regarding the antiquity of the monuments (the actual age of the monuments was not yet known).

An Almost Indifferent Scribe

It is very probably this 'absence of hieroglyphs' that explains Jean-François Champollion's (1790–1832) reaction – a reaction that nevertheless strikes us as surprising. The letter written 'at the foot of the pyramids of Gizeh', on 8 October 1828, the fifth of the thirty-one *Lettres écrites d'Égypte et de*

Opposite top, and above: Belzoni's discovery of the entrance to Khafre's pyramid remains one of the great moments of a pioneering era. Running along almost the entire length of the burial chamber's southern wall (drawing by Belzoni, above, left, and photo, above), the Italian left an inscription – 'Scoperta da G. Belzoni. 2. mar. 1818' – in letters whose size seem to reflect the extent of his disappointment on realizing that he was not the first to enter the chamber. This was evident from the Arabic inscription written in charcoal by one 'Master Mohammed Ahmed, quarrier', who prides himself on having opened the pyramid in the presence of 'Master Othman'. The cross-section of the pyramid is inaccurate: the royal burial chamber was cut out of the bedrock and not part of the body of the masonry.

Nubie en 1828 et 1829, is also the shortest. In this correspondence reflecting the progress of the Franco-Tuscan expedition organized by Champollion and his disciple Ippolito Rosellini, the greatest Egyptologist of them all describes the Pyramids as 'wonders', but is quick to relativize their interest: '[They] need to be studied closely in order to be appreciated fully; they seem to diminish in height the closer one gets to them, and it is only by touching the blocks of stone of which they are composed that one gains a true sense of their mass and their immensity. There is little to be done here, and once we have made copies of the scenes from domestic life sculpted in a tomb near the second pyramid, I shall return to our boats, which are coming to fetch us from Giza, and we shall sail for Upper Egypt, my real headquarters. Thebes is there and we cannot reach it soon enough.' Devoid of inscriptions, the stone mountains were not for the decipherer: what Champollion needed was the challenge of the written text!

The Price of Modernization

As they travelled along the Nile to Wadi Halfa, Champollion and Rosellini experienced at regular intervals what the former describes as 'sharp pangs of regret': where thirty years earlier, exactly, Napoleon's savants had seen monuments that were virtually intact, they found 'only the site' of buildings that in some cases had been demolished barely a few days before their arrival, as in the case of one of the temples of Esna, whose stones had been used 'some twelve days' earlier to reinforce the town quays against the threat of flooding. The price of modernizing the country and of its burgeoning industrialization was the destruction of its ancient buildings, many of which were being reduced to the level of vulgar quarries.

The Great Pyramid narrowly escaped the same awful fate. In his *Mémoires sur*

Below: A portrait of Champollion during the Franco-Tuscan expedition. He was the first to draw the viceroy's attention to the urgent need for safeguarding 'all the different types of monuments that are a continuing testimony to the power and greatness of ancient Egypt, and simultaneously the most beautiful ornaments of modern Egypt'. Champollion's 'Note to the Viceroy on the Conservation of the Monuments of Egypt' was dated November 1829, and on 15 August 1835 Muhammad Ali published a 'superior order' designed to protect Egypt's ancient heritage. It was during this same year, however, that the demolition of the Giza pyramids was due to begin.

NOTE REMISE AU VICE-ROI POUR LA CONSERVATION
DES MONUMENTS DE L'ÉGYPTE.

Alexandrie, novembre 1829.

Parmi les Européens qui visitent l'Égypte, il en est, annuellement, un très-grand nombre qui, n'étant amenés par aucun intérêt commercial, n'ont d'autre désir ou d'autre motif que celui de connaître par eux-mêmes et de contempler les monuments de l'ancienne civilisation égyptienne, monuments épars sur les deux rives du Nil, et que l'on peut aujourd'hui admirer et étudier en toute sûreté, grâce aux sages mesures prises par le gouvernement de Son Altesse.

les principaux travaux d'utilité publique exécutés en Égypte (1872–73), Louis Linant de Bellefonds, Director of Public Works in the time of Muḥammad Ali, recounts how the viceroy, who had published a 'superior order' in 1835 with the aim of protecting Egypt's monuments, had nevertheless decided 'that it was necessary to demolish the Pyramids of Gizeh in order to extract the stones, which would serve in the construction of barrages' at the apex of the Delta.

It was Linant de Bellefonds's quick thinking that saved the pyramids, whose main bulk of rough limestone had been neglected by medieval quarrymen in favour of the much finer limestone of their casing. The Frenchman kept his thoughts to himself regarding 'this deplorable proposition', merely providing a statistical analysis relating to the Great Pyramid alone, which proved that the destruction of the latter and the transportation of stones via a canal that had yet to be dug would cost more than the excavation of a quarry. The project was immediately abandoned.

Curiosity, Perseverance and Gunpowder

It was thanks to two Englishmen, who were only in Egypt for a very short time, that the most important work was carried out at Giza during those years when the pyramids faced, fleetingly, such a major threat.

Above: If we think of the tombs of Khufu, Khafre and Menkaure simply as gigantic piles of stone, it is possible to see how some people could have regarded them merely as convenient quarries where the blocks came ready hewn. Before the pyramids were appreciated as one of the greatest treasures of our cultural heritage, it was only the difference in quality between the fairly coarse limestone core and the much finer limestone casing that saved them from destruction. Medieval quarriers were only interested in the latter and stripped one pyramid after another without really touching the core masonry itself.

Colonel Howard Vyse (1784–1853) arrived in Egypt in 1835 with the idea of systematically exploring the pyramids and obtained the *firman* he needed from Muhammad Ali thanks to the intervention of another colonel, the British consul Campbell, who had agreed to co-finance the works with the vice consul Sloan and Vyse himself. In November 1836, Vyse put Caviglia in charge of the excavations, but Caviglia was determined to do things his own way, ignoring his employer's instructions, and Vyse swiftly replaced him with John Perring (1813–69), a civil engineer who had been engaged for some short while in public works financed by the viceroy. This time the relationship was so good that Vyse had no hesitation in returning to England in August 1837, leaving Perring entirely in charge of the final operations.

Published by Vyse in the form of a journal, although he was not always on site, the *Operations Carried on at the Pyramids of Gizeh in 1837* records the work carried out by Perring on his behalf at the various sites, detailing for each day the number of workmen employed and the programme of works executed. On 14 March, for example, with 7 overseers, 134 men and 127 children, work was simultaneously carried out in several areas of Khufu's pyramid, in Menkaure's pyramid, in two of the small pyramids to the south, at the great Saitic tomb known as 'Campbell's' and in the 'trial passages', a sort of model of the passages of the Great Pyramid situated to the east of the monument.

Perring discovered the second entrance to Khafre's pyramid and the openings of the 'air shafts' in Khufu's burial chamber, but, most importantly, the four other 'stress-relieving chambers' in the Great Pyramid and the entrance to the third pyramid.

The first of Khufu's relieving chambers – 'Davison's chamber', named after the

Below: The architects of Khufu's pyramid devised a scheme for protecting the king's body which involved constructing a series of cavities above the burial chamber. These are known as 'stress-relieving chambers' (section diagram below by Vyse). The first four are roofed with beams similar to those covering the King's Chamber; the fifth has a pented roof, which would in fact have been sufficient to distribute the weight of the masonry above. The structure has suffered serious damage due to subsidence from its own weight.

Englishman who discovered the access to it in 1765 – has a very irregular floor but a ceiling as perfect as the one above the King's Chamber, and it was tempting to ascertain whether a similar space existed above it. Using skilled quarriers from the Mokattam region and (despite the risks) gunpowder, Perring abandoned the sap that Caviglia had attempted to dig towards the south and opened up a vertical shaft. On 29 March, he broke into a new chamber, which he named after the Duke of Wellington, then, continuing his excavations, he reached successively, in April and May, the chambers subsequently named after Lord Nelson, Lady Arbuthnot and Campbell. It was a major discovery and confirmed that the Great Pyramid was indeed the work of Khufu, whose cartouche appeared in several inscriptions uncovered in the chambers.

Since Belzoni had succeeded in opening up Khafre's pyramid, only Menkaure's remained, foiling the efforts of the excavators. Vyse and Perring attacked it in vain,

Above: The average height of the relieving chambers is barely more than a metre, which makes exploring them an experience not dissimilar to potholing. Campbell's Chamber (top) is the only one where it is possible to stand upright. Not many visitors have had the opportunity of entering the chambers since Perring discovered the four upper ones, but graffiti can be seen alongside the marks left, in haematite, by the quarriers. The name of Khufu (bottom) appears several times.

starting from the bottom of the enormous breach that Othman, Saladin's son, had made in the monument's northern face. They dug horizontally, then vertically, towards the heart of the pyramid, but discovered nothing, so they decided to remove the lower part of the granite casing. By basing their calculations, logically enough, on the position of the entrances to the other pyramids, on 28 July 1837 they discovered the opening they were searching for. The burial chamber still contained the broken lid and the intact base of a magnificent 'palace façade' style sarcophagus and, along with some human remains, part of the lid of an anthropoid coffin inscribed with the king's name, but certainly of a late date. This coffin, in which the royal remains must have been reburied after the tomb was desecrated, was removed to the British Museum by Vyse, but the stone base that was to have followed lies at the bottom of the Mediterranean. The boat that was carrying it to England was wrecked somewhere off the coast of Cartagena, Spain.

In 1839, before Vyse even had time to bring out his three-volume work, Perring (who, after Giza, broadened the field of his activities as far as Saqqara) published three large volumes entitled *The Pyramids of Gizeh*, a work admirable for both the precision of its accounts and the extraordinary quality of its plans and sections.

Opposite: Menkaure's burial chamber and the remains of his wooden coffin.

Left: 'Osiris, king of Upper and Lower Egypt, Menkaourê, living for ever, born of the sky, brought forth by Nut, heir of Geb…. Your mother Nut extends over you in her name of "celestial". She ensures that you exist without enemies, king of Upper and Lower Egypt, Menkaourê, living for ever.' This formula, engraved in two columns on the lid of Menkaure's wooden coffin, is taken from the Pyramid Texts, as was common from the 26th dynasty (664–525 BC) onwards – proof that the third pyramid, depicted here, was desecrated at an earlier date and that Menkaure's remains were later reburied, probably by a priest attached to the royal funerary cult, in an anthropoid coffin of a type totally unknown in the Old Kingdom.

A Royal Birthday 'On the Summit'

The pioneering era ended with the Prussian expedition commissioned and financed by King Frederick William IV (1795–1861). Directed on site between 1842 and 1845 by Lepsius, the founder of German Egyptology, the expedition was to be the last major undertaking of its kind and led to the publication of the twelve folio volumes of the *Denkmaeler aus Aegypten und Aethiopien* (1849–59). This was an editorial monument as impressive as the *Description de l'Égypte* – and the only thing that can compare with it – but differs from the latter by the fact that the hieroglyphic texts contained in it have been copied by people who, thanks to Champollion, understood what they saw before them.

Lepsius drew up a map of the Memphite necropolis, from Giza to Saqqara, in which he catalogued sixty-four pyramids which, following excavation, have in some cases turned out to be monuments of a different type. He did not pay special attention, however, to the pyramids at the Giza site, where the great discoveries appeared in any case to be over: for this linguist, following in the footsteps of Champollion, an inscribed mastaba, however modest, appears to have held more interest than a vast monument devoid of inscriptions.

Having chosen the date of 15 October 1842 for his 'first visit to the Great Pyramid' because it was 'His Majesty's birthday', he organized 'a small party in honour [of the] king and of the fatherland' and climbed 'the oldest and highest monument ever constructed by man' in order to fly the Prussian flag and salute 'the Prussian eagle with three cheers for [the] king'. He subsequently left his mark by inscribing the names of the expedition

A bove: This lithograph shows the members of the Prussian expedition, with Lepsius in their midst, celebrating their king's 47th birthday 'on Khufu's pyramid'. The hieroglyphs explain the story.

members in eleven columns of hieroglyphs on one of the sloping beams that overhang the entrance to the Descending Passage.

Opposite: The *Denkmaeler aus Aegypten und Aethiopien* contains 894 large-folio plates (55 x 70 cm) and is a remarkable reference work.

The viceroy Said Pasha marked the end of an era when he signed the order naming the Frenchman Auguste Mariette (1821–81) *mamûr*, or director, of all 'works relating to Egypt's antiquities' on 1 June 1858. The creation of the Antiquities Service put a stop to unauthorized excavations, and henceforth all archaeological fieldwork, whether it related to the pyramids or to little-known sites, became the exclusive prerogative of Egyptologists.

CHAPTER 3

THE SCIENTIFIC ERA

Opposite: Khafre's valley temple, which was cleared by Auguste Mariette. The project marked the start of a period of systematic excavations at Giza, during which a number of important discoveries were made. One of these was the tomb of Queen Hetepheres, Khufu's mother, discovered by George Reisner (right).

One Temple for Another

Mariette took charge of the excavation and conservation of Egypt's ancient monuments, and also set about creating a museum, receiving his authority directly from the viceroy. As soon as he assumed his post at the head of the new Antiquities Service, he began an impressive programme of works which, from Tanis to Elephantine, transformed Egypt into one massive archaeological dig, and in a little over twenty years he attacked more than thirty-five important sites. Giza was one of the first of these. Mariette had already worked there some years earlier with financial support from the Duc de Luynes, but had been obliged to break off before his excavations were complete. In 1853, when work was finished on the Serapeum at Saqqara, his patron had asked him to verify the assertion, as reported by Pliny the Elder, that the Sphinx was composed of foreign materials rather than hewn from the rock on which it stood, and that it was the tomb of a king by the name of Armais. Mariette had therefore set about clearing the sand

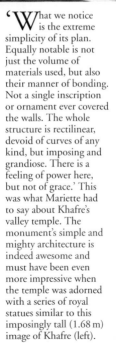

'What we notice is the extreme simplicity of its plan. Equally notable is not just the volume of materials used, but also their manner of bonding. Not a single inscription or ornament ever covered the walls. The whole structure is rectilinear, devoid of curves of any kind, but imposing and grandiose. There is a feeling of power here, but not of grace.' This was what Mariette had to say about Khafre's valley temple. The monument's simple and mighty architecture is indeed awesome and must have been even more impressive when the temple was adorned with a series of royal statues similar to this imposingly tall (1.68 m) image of Khafre (left).

from the immense statue (a task that Caviglia had begun in 1816), had unearthed the Dream Stela and taken several impressions of it and, after a number of soundings, had almost completely excavated the neighbouring 'granite temple', whose function he nevertheless misinterpreted.

Mariette returned to Giza in 1858, although – for reasons that elude us – he began working first in the vicinity of the southernmost of the queens' pyramids situated to the east of Khufu's, which is attributed to a Queen Henutsen. There he uncovered the beautiful sarcophagus belonging to a person by the name of Khufuankh, which was to be one of the jewels in the Boulaq museum collection. Excavations undertaken at the foot of the eastern face of this little pyramid were to prove important for the history of the site by demonstrating that the ancient chapel belonging to the queen's funerary cult was converted, in the New Kingdom (1550–1070 BC), to a temple of Isis under the epithet 'Mistress of the Pyramids'. Here Mariette found the stela known as the Stela of Khufu's Daughter, which he believed to date from the 4th dynasty, but which was in fact an inventory of divine statues, an important document probably dating from the 26th dynasty.

In 1860, Mariette finished excavating the 'granite temple' and made one of his most impressive finds when, in a pit in the vestibule which he took to be 'a water well', he uncovered the magnificent diorite statue representing Khafre under the protection of Horus. Despite the presence of a group of other royal statues, however, he failed to make the connection between the temple and the pyramid and continued to view

Above: This photograph, taken at the north entrance to Khafre's valley temple while the structure was still being cleared, probably dates from 1860. Mariette is wearing the tarboosh commonly worn at the time by Egyptian officials.

Overleaf: A watercolour of the Sphinx produced by Mariette (1853), accompanied by the description of one of Khafre's statues (1860) and inscriptions copied from it.

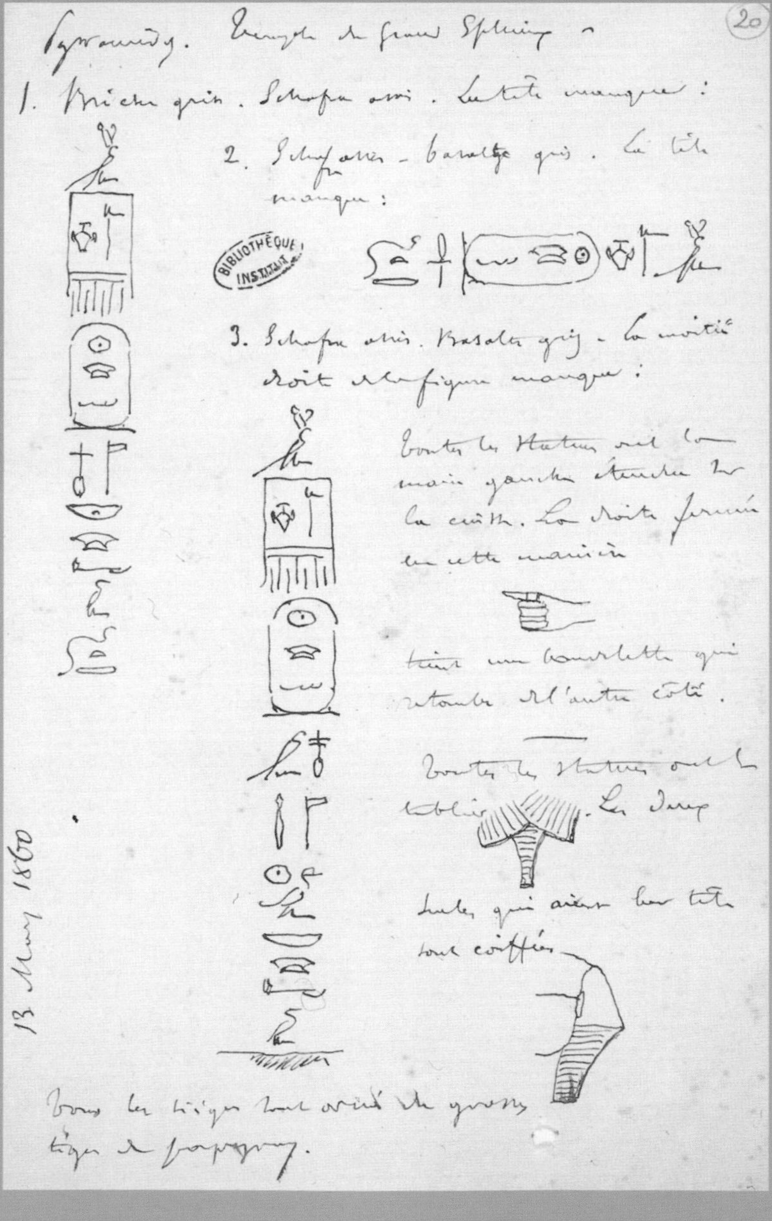

20

Pyramides. Exemple de grand Sphinx.

1. Brèche grise. Schopu avi. La tête manque:

2. Schopu avi - basalte gris. La tête manque:

3. Schopu avis. Basalte gris - la moitié
droite du figure manque:

Toutes les statues ont la
main gauche étendue sur
la cuisse. La droite fermée
en cette manière

tient une tourelette qui
retombe de l'autre côté.

Toutes les statues ont le
tablier ... Les draps

sur les têtes qui avaient leur tête
sont coiffées

Tous les sièges sont ornés de grosses
tiges de papyrus.

the former as the temple of the 'Great Sphinx', asking himself: 'Is the monument in fact an annexe of the Sphinx or the Sphinx an annexe of the monument?' It was not until some forty years later that the 'granite temple' would be identified as the valley temple of Khafre's pyramid complex.

From Stonehenge to Giza

In 1865, Charles Piazzi Smyth (1819–1900), Astronomer Royal of Scotland and Professor of Astronomy at the University of Edinburgh, set about recording precise measurements of the Great Pyramid. Despite his eminent scientific qualifications, Piazzi Smyth adhered to the theories propounded by John Taylor according to which the builders of the Great Pyramid – necessarily inspired by God – calculated the dimensions of the monument using a 'pyramid inch', supposedly the five hundred millionth part of the earth's diameter. Although the 'sacred cubit' (*c.* 63.5 cm) and its supposed twenty-five pyramid inches were pure figments of his imagination, Piazzi Smyth nevertheless succeeded in producing extremely precise surveys, particularly inside the colossal structure.

Above: This photograph, taken from the Great Pyramid's original entrance looking east, shows the measuring rods placed by Piazzi Smyth perpendicularly to the base of the monument and to the slope of the Descending Passage. By determining that the angle between the axis of the passage and the horizontal was 26° 26′ 46″, Smyth was able to demonstrate the orientation of the Descending Passage towards Alpha Draconis – the Pole Star of that time.

Left: Petrie at the entrance to the rock tomb where he lived during the two seasons that he devoted to the triangulation of the Giza pyramids (1880–82).

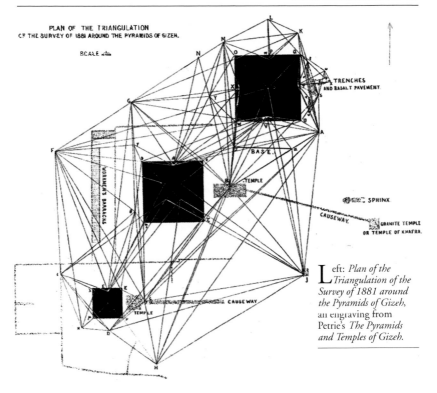

PLAN OF THE TRIANGULATION
OF THE SURVEY OF 1881 AROUND THE PYRAMIDS OF GIZEH.

SCALE

Left: Plan of the Triangulation of the Survey of 1881 around the Pyramids of Gizeh, an engraving from Petrie's *The Pyramids and Temples of Gizeh.*

His published findings were to have at least one important consequence, moreover, inspiring the thirteen-year-old Flinders Petrie, that indefatigable excavator who has come to be regarded as 'the father of Egyptology'. It was reading Piazzi Smyth's *Our Inheritance in the Great Pyramid* (1864) and *Life and Work at the Great Pyramid* (1867) that first sparked and later affirmed Petrie's interest in ancient Egypt and its monuments, beginning with those at Giza.

By assisting his father, a civil engineer and surveyor, Petrie had learnt how to carry out topographical surveys and had worked on several sites in Britain, including Stonehenge, one of Europe's most important megalithic monuments. Petrie was given the task of calculating the measurements of the three pyramids trigonometrically –

a method that had not been used previously but which was the only one that could be relied upon to produce precise results, since the base of the pyramid was still encumbered with debris and a straightforward survey was therefore impossible. Petrie devoted two six-month stints to the project between December 1880 and April 1882, during which time he lodged in one of the rock tombs and enlisted the help of Ali Gabri, an Egyptian intimately acquainted with the area who had worked as a child with Vyse and later with Piazzi Smyth. The year 1883 saw the publication of his *The Pyramids and Temples of Gizeh*, which includes the first bibliography of books and articles relating to the region, totalling a thousand titles.

In addition to the measurements taken using three different theodolites, a goniometer and a sextant, the work contains a record of Petrie's operations in the region and the various observations he was able to make, in particular regarding the Great Pyramid. After clearing the Descending Passage once more, he queried the manner of sealing the pyramids and the nature of the 'movable stone' mentioned by Strabo. And having taken very precise measurements (more so than elsewhere) in the King's Chamber, he notes that all the granite ceiling beams are broken and concludes from this that the collapse of the entire structure can only be a matter of time and of earth tremors.

Above: The first European travellers often saw only the head of the Sphinx emerging from the desert sands. The structure was cleared on several separate occasions over the years. Here, we see it in *c.* 1870, prior to the last excavation in the 19th century.

Sharing Out an Immense Necropolis

As director of the Antiquities Service, Mariette had been the only person to excavate the site of the great pyramids for more than twenty years. Following his death in 1881, his successor Gaston Maspero, who particularly admired the work carried out at Giza by Petrie, granted the latter virtually exclusive rights to excavate the site. Between 1887 and 1891, Petrie abandoned Giza for other pyramid sites, visiting successively Illahun, Hawara and Meidum.

Maspero organized for clearance work to continue on the Sphinx in 1886 and was now eager for the various parts of the site to be excavated simultaneously by a number of foreign missions, the idea being that each of them would be granted certain concessions – a situation that was successfully negotiated in the course of a meeting held in 1902 and attended by the German Ludwig Borchardt, professor at the University of Leipzig, on behalf of Georg Steindorff, the Italian Ernesto Schiaparelli, Director of Turin's Museum of Antiquities, and the American George Reisner, originally Director of the Hearst Egyptian Expedition of the University of California and later Director of the Joint Egyptian Expedition of Harvard University and the Boston Museum of Fine Arts. The sector comprising Khafre's pyramid and part of the cemetery situated to the north of it fell to Borchardt. Schiaparelli was granted another part of the same cemetery, known as the 'Western Cemetery' (in relation to the Great Pyramid),

The Dream Stela still stands between the Sphinx's paws (opposite) and tells how the future Thutmose IV fell asleep there during a hunting expedition and saw the Sphinx in a dream, and how the latter promised to give him 'royalty' if he would free it 'from the desert sand' that 'advanced towards' it. The first known excavation of the colossal statue took place, therefore, during the 18th dynasty, in c. 1400 BC, since the stela is dated from the first year of Thutmose's reign. Several other excavations followed, including one carried out under the aegis of Gaston Maspero (left), but the desert sands would swiftly encroach again, to the point, perhaps, of sometimes covering the huge statue completely, as suggested by the fact that certain classical authors appear not to have seen it. The Sphinx was totally and definitively excavated in 1926 and has since been the object of several restorations. Eroded parts of the monument have been replaced with blocks of limestone which give the impression, in particular as regards the paws and the hindquarters, that rather than being sculpted the statue was constructed piece by piece.

while Reisner's concession included the whole of Menkaure's funerary complex, together with the northern and southern fringes of the Western Cemetery and also the cemetery situated to the east of Khufu's pyramid.

Fortune's Favourite

The members of all these commissions made discoveries as numerous as they were remarkable, but – without in any way detracting from his unflagging efforts as an excavator – George Reisner had, in the true sense of the word and on two separate occasions, more luck than

the others: when lots were first drawn, Reisner won the concession to excavate Menkaure's pyramid, and it was later thanks to the greatest piece of good fortune that his team discovered the tomb of Queen Hetepheres, mother of Khufu.

Since the smallest of the three pyramids – which, in terms of volume, is less than a tenth the size of Khufu's – was well known to archaeologists thanks to the work of Vyse and Perring, Reisner focused instead on elements of the pyramid complex, which revealed itself to be relatively better developed than those of Khufu or Khafre. From 1906 to 1924, with interruptions due to work he was carrying out simultaneously in Nubia and Sudan, Reisner excavated in turn the mortuary temple, situated up against the eastern face of the pyramid, the causeway linking this temple to the valley temple (today inaccessible), the chapels

Fragments of a royal colossus (left) were uncovered in Menkaure's mortuary temple. The restored statue (below) is in Boston's Museum of Fine Arts.

belonging to the three queens' pyramids, and finally the field of mastabas belonging to the funerary priests associated with the royal cult.

Excavation of the mortuary temple, constructed from blocks of local limestone, the largest of which weighs over two hundred tons, demonstrated that the cult complex, which was still incomplete at the time of Menkaure's death, was finished in mudbrick by his successor Shepseskaf. A variety of archaeological materials, including flint blades, amulets and Greek coins, were discovered – proof that the site was re-used – and, in addition to these, the remains of a larger-than-life calcite statue of the seated king which must have been located at the heart of his temple.

Clearance of the valley temple produced surprises of a different kind, comparable to those Mariette had uncovered in Khafre's 'granite temple': the intact statues which Reisner discovered here rank among the masterpieces of Egyptian sculpture. Alongside a significant

Above: The discovery of Menkaure's intact triads in 1908, while Reisner was working on the valley temple, represents one of Egyptian archaeology's finest moments. The remains, in some cases badly fragmented, of other similar groupings representing the king with Hathor and a deity personifying a nome suggest that there were probably as many statues as there were administrative divisions of Egypt (at least thirty at the time). With the exception of these few, all have disappeared.

number of fragments, Reisner found a magnificent effigy of the royal couple and no fewer than four triads representing the king accompanied by the goddess Hathor and a deity personifying one of the Egyptian nomes or administrative regions.

Hetepheres' tomb – a hiding place rather than a sepulchre, since the queen's body was not found there – was discovered by chance in 1925 when one of the feet of a photographer's tripod sank into the ground, revealing the presence of a shaft more than 27 metres deep.

Ceaseless Activity

Other missions – under the direction of the German Hermann Junker and of the Egyptians Selim Hassan and Abdel-Moneim Abu Bakr – continued to focus on Giza up until the 1950s. These were not directly concerned with the three pyramids, but only with the tombs of private individuals surrounding the monuments or situated in the vicinity of the Sphinx.

Junker, a professor at the University of Vienna, worked on the central part of the Western Cemetery. From 1912 to 1914 and from the end of the Great War up until 1929, he systematically excavated a vast sector, recording

Below: On 17 April 1927, the alabaster sarcophagus belonging to Queen Hetepheres was raised up from a shaft discovered by chance two years earlier. This photograph is taken looking north–north-east, between the northernmost of the queens' pyramids (left) and the mastaba belonging to Kawab, Khufu's eldest son (right). Behind the hut that shelters the entrance to the shaft, and across the whole width of the photograph, we can just make out the slightly paler sloping line showing where the causeway ran between the Great Pyramid's valley and mortuary temples (which have now disappeared).

his findings in a dozen publications which appeared between 1929 and 1955 and make an important contribution to our knowledge of the site. From 1929 onwards, Selim Hassan, the first Egyptian to be appointed Professor of Egyptology at the University of Cairo, concentrated his efforts on the Central Field, in other words the area south of the Sphinx and Khafre's causeway, clearing the mastabas, but also the Sphinx itself and the temples dedicated to its cult. Thanks to his efforts, the huge statue would never be buried by the sands again. Then, in 1938–39, he dedicated his final campaign to the southern and eastern faces of the Great Pyramid, focusing in particular on the remains of the mortuary temple. Between 1949 and 1953, Abdel-Moneim Abu Bakr, professor at the University of Alexandria, excavated a series of 5th- and 6th-dynasty (2465–2150 BC) tombs located in the north-west of the huge Western Cemetery, near the small area explored in 1915 by the American Clarence Fisher.

Above: Hetepheres's splendid burial goods were very poorly preserved. Almost all the wooden components had totally decomposed, and sorting through them was to prove a long and painstaking job. In this photograph, taken in 1926, Noel Wheeler lies on a mattress contemplating the task before him as if unsure where to begin.

Queen Hetepheres's 'tomb' is an enigma, and we will probably never know the truth about it. Though we call it a tomb, it is in fact merely a hiding place without a superstructure in which, at some indeterminate date, all or part of the queen's funerary goods were stashed – but not her body. Khufu's mother was the wife of Sneferu and would almost certainly have been buried at Dahshur, and it is possible that her real tomb was looted and her body removed. The cache at Giza was discovered at the bottom of a shaft, 27 metres deep, situated close to Khufu's causeway, in a chamber little more than 5 metres long, less than 3 metres wide and just under 2 metres high (opposite, top). It contained a canopic chest and an alabaster sarcophagus surrounded by an assortment of burial goods made of wood decorated with gold foil: poles belonging to a type of canopy and a long box designed to hold curtains for it (left), two sitting chairs, a bed, a carrying chair (opposite), jewelry caskets (this page, top: photograph of excavated materials, including bangles, shown below following restoration), gold and alabaster vessels, and pieces of pottery.

In 1954, clearance work in the vicinity of the Great Pyramid led to the discovery of two sealed pits, one of which was subsequently opened. The pit was 30 metres long and 5 metres deep and covered with a roof of 41 limestone slabs set edgewise (opposite). Inscriptions in red and black ink on their lower faces (opposite, bottom) indicate that the slabs were placed there by Khufu's son Djedefre. Inside the pit was a perfectly preserved boat made up of 1,224 pieces of wood, all cut from cedars of Lebanon with the exception of a few pieces of acacia wood. The pieces had been laid in thirteen superimposed layers and ranged in size from a few centimetres to 23 metres, all held together by ropes woven from fibres of esparto grass. The reassembled boat (left and above) measured 43.4 metres in length and 5.9 metres at its widest point and had five pairs of oars and two steering oars.

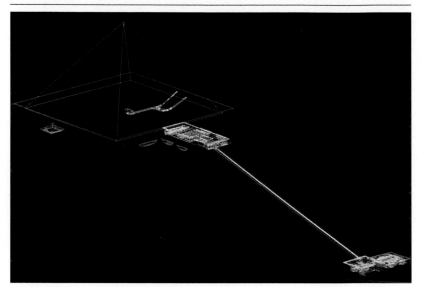

Decades of excavation and related work had by no means exhausted the site of the great pyramids and new discoveries continued to be made, sometimes of an exceptional nature, as was the case in 1954 with the famous discovery of 'Khufu's boats'. While excavated materials were being cleaned between the southern face of the Great Pyramid and the row of later mastaba tombs that lie alongside it, two long sealed pits were discovered containing two huge disarticulated boats. Only the eastern pit was opened up and the huge slabs covering it were removed. It contained an elegant cedar wood barque, which has been magnificently restored by master craftsman Ahmed Youssef and can now be admired in its own specially built museum.

Similarly, in 1991, while the tarmac road along the Great Pyramid's eastern face was being removed to prevent tourist buses from damaging the remains of the basalt pavement of Khufu's mortuary temple, Zahi Hawass, Secretary General of the Supreme Council of Antiquities, found the remains of a small satellite pyramid and its pyramidion between the Great Pyramid's southeastern angle and the southernmost of the three queens' pyramids.

Above: A great number of Egyptian monuments are so well preserved that they require no effort of the imagination. Sometimes, however, the terrain can only be 'read' as a result of patient restorations: many Egyptologists would have trouble understanding the organization of Djoser's funerary complex, built at Saqqara in the 3rd dynasty (2649–2575 BC), had J.-P. Lauer not spent decades producing an anastylosis of its principal elements. Today 3D modelling enables us to visualize immediately the layout of a pyramid complex such as Khafre's.

A year earlier, during drainage works at Nazlet el-Samman, below the plateau, a basalt wall was discovered in a trench where pipes were due to be laid. Given the topography of the region, the wall, which was 56 metres long, must have belonged to the valley temple in Khufu's funerary complex. In 1993, while foundations were being excavated on a building site a little further to the east, a section of wall was discovered, this time part of the harbour belonging to the same complex.

Excavations carried out since the beginning of the 1990s serve, finally, as a prosaic reminder that Giza's

mythical monuments are the work of human hands – despite all the 'mysteries' that are still obstinately attached to them in certain quarters. During work on behalf of the Giza Plateau Mapping Project, directed by the American Mark Lehner, Lehner himself discovered the sector where the workers lived, and Zahi Hawass the cemetery where they were buried. Beyond the great 'Wall of the Crow', which appears to have been the southern limit of the royal necropolis itself, bakeries and areas for drying fish have been uncovered, along with workshops and warehouses, that reveal something of the daily lives of those who worked to prepare a life in the hereafter for their kings before themselves being buried in modest mudbrick tombs.

Left: In 1954, after more than a century of excavations, Khufu's boat pits were discovered quite by chance, and similarly, in 1991, traces of his satellite pyramid (the first two courses of which can be seen in this photograph). Such discoveries remind us that, while parts of the Giza plateau have yet to be cleared down to the bedrock, important finds are still possible (quite apart from the mastaba tombs awaiting excavation). In the case of Menkaure's pyramid alone, more than half of the base is still concealed by enormous piles of granite, and it is tempting to wonder whether more boat pits might come to light when these casing remains are cleared. None have been found at the foot of this pyramid to date.

'It is clear moreover that the ground on which these pyramids are erected served the ancient Egyptians as a cemetery, and that the pyramids were mausoleums and tombs destined to receive the bodies of the Pharaohs, the important members of their court, and those responsible for their construction, since in addition to the three large ones of which I shall speak further and which are the most famous, there are a fair number of other small ones […], not to mention certain very long sepulchres of perpendicular design, built of neatly hewn stones […].'

Anthoine Morison, *Voyage en Égypte*, 1697

CHAPTER 4
THE CEMETERY COMPLEX

Opposite: Pyramids and mastabas are merely superstructures – on a very different scale from one another – erected over individual tombs. In the pyramid, the tomb is reached via a series of passages, and in the mastaba via a shaft, as clearly indicated by this 3D plan (right).

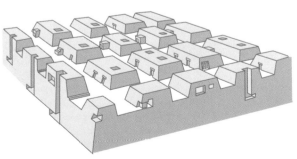

In his *Itinéraire des invités*, produced for the benefit of important guests attending the inauguration of the Suez Canal, Auguste Mariette wrote of the pyramids: 'We do violence to all that we know of Egypt, and to all that archaeology has taught us with regard to that country's monumental practices, by viewing them as anything but tombs.' Mariette was merely repeating what had seemed self-evident to travellers down the centuries who, like Anthoine Morison, possessed sufficient independence of mind to dismiss the more outlandish notions pertaining to the pyramids. Morison, a highly educated canon from Lorraine in eastern France, was correct in supposing that

the 'very long sepulchres' (or mastabas) were tombs of high officials, but he could not have guessed that 'the sand which the wind has piled around them' also concealed constructions of a different type.

A Triple Funerary Complex

Each of the great pyramids, whose massive bulk eclipses everything in its vicinity, is in fact only the most visible part of a monumental complex of varying size where we find, transposed to the royal level, the two principal elements of the mastaba type: the 'eternal dwelling place' of the dead person, in other words the burial vault and tomb, and the chapel where rituals were enacted in the dead person's name and where offerings were left.

Left: This aerial photograph showing Menkaure's pyramid from the south-east demonstrates the relatively large size of the mortuary temple vis-à-vis the pyramid itself. We can also see how blocks of granite dislodged from the casing have created a substantial pile of rubble concealing the base of the pyramid and its immediate approaches.

Giza is an exceptional site with three contiguous complexes whose various elements (some better conserved than others) command our attention in different ways. The pyramid or royal tomb evolved from the simple pit grave surmounted by a mound of earth and stones, typical of the pre-dynastic period. In addition to its pyramid, each complex comprises a mortuary or upper temple built against the monument's eastern side, and a valley or lower temple serving as a portal to the entire complex and situated, as its name suggests, below the desert plateau, near a funerary 'harbour', and linked to the mortuary temple by a sloping causeway several hundred metres long. The best-preserved cult complex is Khafre's, but because of the absence of any kind of

A bove: This reconstruction of the triple funerary complex at Giza owes a great deal to excavations carried out at Abusir between 1902 and 1908 by the German Ludwig Borchardt, whose work on the pyramids of Sahure, Neferirkare and Niuserre – pharaohs of the 5th dynasty – revealed how the various elements of a pyramid complex fitted together.

decoration, in either the 'granite temple' or the mortuary temple, we cannot be certain what ceremonies took place there. It was originally supposed that the king was mummified in the valley temple and that rites were celebrated in the mortuary temple prior to the actual funeral, but it now seems more likely that the valley temple served as a setting for purification rites, and that it was in the mortuary temple that the cult of the dead king was perpetuated after his burial. Later, when the pharaohs of the New Kingdom separated their tombs – hollowed out of the rock in the Valley of the Kings – from the 'temples of millions of years' situated at the edge of the desert, it was the latter that fulfilled this cult role.

Secondary pyramids and boat pits (although none have yet been found for Menkaure's pyramid) completed the pyramid complex and were located near the king's pyramid, within an area that was marked out by modest enclosure walls. The small pyramids belonging to the kings' wives are not to be confused with the even smaller, single pyramid known as a 'satellite' or 'subsidiary' pyramid, whose symbolic function is still not entirely clear to us. The boat pits can be divided into two types: boat-shaped pits, which may merely have served to represent boats rather than necessarily containing real ones (five such are to be found in the vicinity

Above: The pyramids belonging to Menkaure's queens are aligned to the south of the king's tomb, whereas Khufu's wives were buried to the east of the Great Pyramid.

Below: A beautiful private sarcophagus, devoid of inscriptions but carved in 'palace façade' style, from one of the mastabas in the Eastern Cemetery.

of Khufu's pyramid), and rectangular-shaped pits containing the disarticulated sections of entire boats, which would not have fitted in the space in their assembled form. The hermetically sealed pits discovered in 1954 are examples of the latter.

And finally, although not strictly a part of the pyramid complex, there were the private cemeteries lying alongside the pyramids, in particular Khufu's. Some of

Below: In this low-angle shot, taken from the top of the monument, we are looking down the Great Pyramid's southeastern edge. A handful of mastabas in the Eastern Cemetery and the three queens' pyramids can be seen in the top left

these mastabas are very large and their regularly aligned rows form what looks like a grid of streets at the foot of the gigantic tomb (royal family to the east, important officials to the west). Together with the Great Pyramid and its three queens' pyramids, all these tombs present, as if frozen in stone, the image of a highly hierarchical society dominated by the pharaonic institution. The three pyramids at Giza, to which the Egyptians generally gave the title borne by their respective owners, mark the high point of this type of royal tomb and stand out from all the rest.

corner and, on the near side of the tarmac road, a boat pit and the site where the remains of Khufu's satellite pyramid were found. The oblong building to the right houses the cedarwood boat uncovered in 1954. Napoleon's savants assumed that the line of tombs which it partially obscures were small pyramids.

The richly decorated mastabas belonging to members of the royal family – such as Prince Khufukhaf's (opposite) and Queen Meresankh's (left) – are located in the Eastern Cemetery. Archaeologists have known about these for many years, but some of the private tombs in the Western Cemetery have yet to be excavated. Work is continuing in the westernmost part of the cemetery under the aegis of the Supreme Council of Antiquities and has led to some splendid discoveries, such as this statue of the priest Kay (below).

'The Horizon of Khufu'

The tomb known as 'the Horizon of Khufu', second king of the 4th dynasty, is a unique monument that justifies, more than either of its two neighbours, every superlative that has ever been applied to it. Everything about it is exceptional, including the sheer scale of its construction and the arrangement of its internal parts.

We only have to look at the figures to understand how the Great Pyramid should have assumed its mythical status. With its base length of 230.34 metres and its original height of 146.6 metres – in round figures, 440 and 280 cubits, where one cubit equals

B elow: The Great Pyramid, seen from the north-west.

B ottom: It is ironic that the only effigy of Khufu to be clearly identified is this tiny ivory statuette (7.5 cm), discovered at Abydos by Petrie. Two or three larger heads, including the Sphinx head, may in fact be attributable to the same pharaoh.

0.5235 metres – Khufu's pyramid has a volume of 2,592,340 m³ and covers more than five hectares. Its angle of slope is 51° 50′ 34″, since it was constructed using a ratio of 14:11, which is the ratio of the sides of the right-angled triangle formed by its height and half its base length.

Apart from the basalt pavement, discovered by J.-P. Lauer in 1949, which is all that remains of the mortuary temple, and traces of the sloping causeway, whose decorative elements were described by Herodotus, almost nothing remains of the principal elements of Khufu's

funerary complex. The ruins of the valley temple and its port lie beneath the dwellings of the modern town of Nazlet el-Samman, built below the level of the plateau – as indicated by recent discoveries that were to prove as fugitive as they were fortuitous, since we have nothing to show for them. This absence of remains is in no way surprising: blocks likely to have originated from Khufu's causeway were re-used to build the core of Amenemhet I's pyramid at Lisht, proof that the secondary elements of the Great Pyramid complex started to be re-employed as materials elsewhere from the 12th dynasty (1991–1783 BC) onwards.

Above: The Grand Gallery is a stupendous achievement, almost 48 metres long and 8.6 metres high, all the more surprising after the cramped and difficult crawl up the narrow Ascending Passage. It rises at the same angle, its walls made up of a series of seven corbels that form the most elegant nave.

The most intriguing aspect of the Great Pyramid – more intriguing even than its colossal size or the 'mysteries' and skilfulness of its construction – is its internal structure, and it is this that also accounts, in large part, for the monument's mythical status.

There are not just one, but in fact three funerary apartments here, laid out in a goose-foot formation. Was this arrangement the result of a definitive and unified plan, as Rainer Stadelmann thinks, or is Ludwig Borchardt (and, following him, the majority of Egyptologists) correct in assuming that it corresponded to three separate initiatives? The fact that the first dozen or so metres of the Ascending Passage have been hollowed out of

B elow: Khufu's three burial chambers reveal changes of plan in the course of construction, and the internal layout of his tomb is a great deal more complex than that of any other pyramid. This cross-section shows:
1. Casing (lost)
2. Entrance
3. Descending Passage (constructed section)
4. Junction of passages and granite plugs
5. Descending Passage (excavated section)
6. Subterranean Chamber
7. Well
8. Ascending Passage

horizontal beds of masonry, the unfinished state of the so-called 'air shafts' originating in the Queen's Chamber and the sinking of the evacuation well, apparently as an after-thought, all confirm that changes of plan did undoubtedly occur in the course of construction.

There are a great many questions that have still to be answered or have given rise to a variety of contradictory answers. What, for example, is the real purpose of the 'air shafts', in particular those that led from the Queen's

9. Horizontal passage
10. 'Queen's' Chamber (so-called)
11. 'Air shafts' (so-called)
12. Grand Gallery
13. Antechamber
14. King's Chamber
15. 'Relieving' chambers
16. Breach made by al-Mamun (access to Ascending Passage)

Chamber without actually opening to the outside, and which were obstructed at the level of the chamber itself? What is the purpose of the astonishing piece of construction known as the Grand Gallery? Why is the King's Chamber heavily offset south from the centre axis, and why is it surmounted by these 'stress-relieving chambers', thought to be unique until the discovery of similar cavities in the Meidum pyramid?

Finally, the debate continues about how and when the Great Pyramid was looted, or simply opened up. Some of the evidence is contradictory. The fact that Strabo speaks of a 'movable stone' with, behind it, 'a sloping gallery leading down to the tomb' does not signify that the remaining passages and chambers were known at that time: the bottom of the Ascending Passage is still blocked today by granite plugs, and the only way to reach the upper areas would have been to use the well – the escape route necessarily taken by workmen after sealing the tomb. If Strabo had heard of the other passages and chambers, would he not have mentioned them?

Moreover, for al-Mamun's men, seeking a way into the pyramid, to have made their famous breach (logically enough) in the monument's axis at the level of the sixth course (whereas the actual entrance was located 7.2 metres further over to the east and ten courses higher) the latter must in fact have been totally invisible, and therefore carefully sealed again following Strabo's visit (assuming we can trust his evidence). If this was the case,

Left: The relative positions of the Great Pyramid's two 'entrances' are clearly visible in this photograph: in the centre, the original entrance opening into the passage that leads down to the unfinished chamber cut out of the rock; lower down, to the right, the breach made by al-Mamun, which connects with the Ascending Passage. At the bottom we can see the only intact fragment of casing still in place at the level of the first course of masonry.

Below: This shot was taken at the junction of the al-Mamun breach and the Ascending Passage, looking towards the latter. To the right are some modern steps leading up towards the Grand Gallery; to the left two of the three granite plugs that blocked the access to the upper galleries.

when must such an initiative have taken place, and on whose orders? It could have been instigated by Septimius Severus, who, according to Cassius Dio (*Roman History*, LXXVI, 13), ordered that all the sacred books removed from Egyptian temples should be shut inside Alexander's tomb. Might he have done the same thing when he sealed up the Great Pyramid after visiting it in 200? This is clearly no more than a hypothesis, but we may have the seeds here of the Surid legend, according to which the pyramids served both 'as a repository for scientific knowledge and as tombs *for* the bodies of kings'.

Below: Khafre's mortuary temple is badly ruined and, for most of its length, there are no more than traces of the causeway that connected the mortuary temple to the valley temple, which, by contrast, is well conserved (foreground).

'Khafre Is Great'

The tomb belonging to Khufu's second son was very similar to his father's, in terms of its dimensions at least. The fact that the bases of the two monuments are at distinctly different levels, added to the fact that Khafre's has retained the upper part of its casing, even creates the illusion today that his tomb is larger than Khufu's. Its original volume was 2,217,000 m³ and it has a sharper angle of slope (53° 7' 48"), which it owes to a ratio of 4:3 between its height (143.5 metres) and half of its base measurement (215.3 metres).

Khafre's pyramid differs from Khufu's in terms of its casing, the first course of which, at least, was in red Aswan granite, but the overriding difference relates to the arrangement and positioning of his funerary apartment. Despite its double entrance, this is very much less complex than Khufu's and essentially hewn out of the bedrock, below ground level. The same was true for the tomb of Khafre's predecessor and half-brother, Djedefre, at Abu Roash, and would be the rule for all future pyramids.

It was a German mission directed by Ernst von Sieglin in 1909–10 that uncovered the remains of Khafre's imposing mortuary temple, and restorations carried out by Uvo Hölscher demonstrated that the previously paved and covered causeway provided a link between this and the still more imposing temple – described by Auguste Mariette as the 'Sphinx Temple' – which was referred to henceforth simply as Khafre's 'valley temple'.

Left: Cross-section of Khafre's burial chamber. Following serious structural problems, which almost led to the collapse of Khufu's burial vault, the architects of his successors' tombs never risked constructing even the most modest funerary chamber within the core masonry of a pyramid again. Khafre's burial chamber was not set as deeply as Djedefre's at Abu Roash, but was located just beneath the pyramid's structural mass, with the pented beams of its roof resting directly on the bedrock.

Below: Detail of the statue of Khafre seated on his throne.

'Menkaure Is Divine'

Menkaure's sepulchre is altogether a more modest structure and owes its inclusion among the great pyramids to its location alongside Khufu's and Khafre's. The tomb builders had reckoned on a height of 125 cubits and a base length of 200 cubits, but the final monument was only 65.5 metres high with a slightly irregular base of approximately

Left: This portrait of Menkaure, in beautiful white Egyptian alabaster, was found in his valley temple and is now conserved in Boston. What makes it unusual is the lack of headdress of any kind, the king's rank being indicated merely by his beard and by the uraeus rising up from his short hair.

105 metres, giving the structure a volume of slightly more than 240,000 m³ – less than a tenth of the volume of the Great Pyramid, whose angle of slope it almost shares, since the ratio of 5:4 used here gives a 51° 20′ 24″ angle.

The monument's originality lies in its intact casing of red granite, which led Arabic writers to describe it

Above: This antechamber with its walls carved in 'palace façade' style is a testimony to the work of the ancient quarrymen who hollowed out funerary apartments from the solid rock.

as 'painted' or 'coloured'. The original intention was probably to encase the entire structure in the same stone, quarried some distance away at Aswan, but the task was never completed. Instead, Menkaure's son and successor Shepseskaf finished the casing more cheaply, and possibly in something of a hurry, using blocks of limestone coated in a haematite-based paint – as was proved by analyses carried out in 1993 by Gilles Dormion and Jean-Yves Verd'hurt, under the direction of Chawki Nakhla – which gave the entire pyramid a reddish hue, justifying the epithets used by Arab writers. Now that the layer of fine limestone is missing, the enormous vertical breach left in the centre of the northern side by Saladin's son reveals the stepped structure at the heart of the monument. One final thing worth noting is the size of the mortuary temple (which is much more complex in design than Khufu's) in relation to the size of the pyramid, as if the builders were attempting to compensate for its modest scale.

The lower section of Menkaure's pyramid casing (above right) was composed of 16 courses of red granite, 'rough laid' throughout, except around the entrance, beneath the breach (above left). At the back of the latter is the passage opened by Vyse and Perring, shown on the cross-section below.

The Sphinx is the guardian of the pyramids and matches them for size, being 72 metres long and 20 metres high. Hewn from local limestone that has been eroded by the wind to reveal successive strata of varying hardness, it is the largest and oldest statue of a sphinx – the name given by the Greeks to a hybrid creature combining a lion's body and a human head. First and foremost an image of royal power, the Sphinx (called by the Arabs Abu al-Hol, 'Father of Terror') also carries solar connotations, as affirmed by its identification with the god Harmakhis, the sun 'in the horizon', from the 18th dynasty onwards. It has long been assumed that the statue represents Khafre, although its face, which is both wider and more angular, bears no resemblance to Khafre's. Several factors, in particular the original absence of a beard, and the fact that the Sphinx is located in the quarry used by Khufu, suggests that it may in fact represent Khufu and not Khafre.

ARRÊTANT SON CHEVAL AU PIED DE LA GRANDE PYRAMIDE, MORTIMER LÈVE PENSIVEMENT LES YEUX SUR LE GIGANTESQUE TOMBEAU DU PHARAON KHÉOPS...

Dire que le mot de l'énigme est peut-être là, à portée de la main... Oui, tout me dit que cette montagne de pierre n'a pas livré tous ses secrets et que le papyrus de Manéthon doit répondre à une réalité... La chambre d'Horus existe !... Je le sens !...

'There are countless people who quite seriously [imagine] Khufu's pyramid to be a place where arcane knowledge is concealed. And since the pyramid is utterly devoid of inscriptions that might otherwise contain such teachings, these fanatics suppose that the latter must be expressed by some other means. It is in the measurements of the various parts of the pyramid that revelation apparently lies.'

Adolf Erman

CHAPTER 5

THESES, HYPOTHESES AND REALITIES

Opposite: Edgar P. Jacobs's *Le Mystère de la Grande Pyramide* is in many respects a more plausible fiction than the majority of works relating to what might loosely be termed 'pyramidology', some of which (right) have set out to prove fanciful theories, including the instrumental role of the Atlanteans in the construction of the Great Pyramid!

In the 1930s, the great German Egyptologist Adolf Erman poured scorn on those he described as 'fanatics' and thoroughly discredited their 'daft ideas' regarding the Great Pyramid. Erman would probably be astonished, however, to realize that, despite a further three quarters of a century of research, those fanatics are still alive and well, and producing a steady stream of articles and books positing the most eccentric theories – not to mention the pseudo-scientific documentaries being broadcast by various television channels. He would be interested to note that it is still the Great Pyramid, and only the Great Pyramid, which is the focus of so much attention and the source of so many surprising notions.

The Various Theories

For classical authors, the pyramids at Giza were tombs, quite simply and clearly, and their identification with 'Joseph's granaries' contained no cryptic subtext. Even in Arabic legends, they were royal burial places, albeit also repositories for hieratic knowledge and wisdom. But for some people Khufu's pyramid is anything but a royal tomb, and in the mid-19th century in Europe there emerged a host of theories developing various blends of mysticism and pseudo-science.

John Taylor's book, *The Great Pyramid: Why Was It Built? and Who Built It?*, published in 1859, was the first to put forward 'biblical' theories. Since the people who built the pyramids did not possess the knowledge, mathematical or otherwise, necessary for the construction of these monuments, Taylor argued, they must have gained their inspiration from God and must therefore belong to the chosen race. The astronomer Charles Piazzi Smyth espoused many of Taylor's ideas and did much to help diffuse them by attempting to

Above: This curious imaginary view, dated 1891, seems to have been inspired by the theories of Richard Proctor, who believed that Khufu's pyramid was originally built as an observatory. It shows a cross-section of the Grand Gallery and two astronomer–priests studying the stars in the southern sky, visible through its upper opening.

prove, among other things, that the ancient Egyptians knew the value of π and that they had used a 'pyramid inch' corresponding to the five hundred millionth part of the Earth's diameter.

Partly in order to refute these theories, in 1883 another astronomer, Richard Proctor, published a book entitled *The Great Pyramid*, in which, taking up one of Jomard's ideas, he explains that the pyramid was initially no more than an observatory, and continued as such for a considerable period of time. According to Proctor, the initial construction ended at the fiftieth course of masonry, at the level of the King's Chamber, and the Descending Passage and Grand Gallery were deliberately angled towards the stars Alpha Draconis and Alpha Centauri, respectively. Only later did Khufu finish building the pyramid in order to turn it into his private tomb.

In the 20th century, David Davidson took up the relay with *The Great Pyramid, Its Divine Message, an Original Co-ordination of Historical Documents and Archaeological Evidences*, published in 1924, a substantial work providing an impressive number of tables and figures,

Below: This early 20th-century postcard shows a cross-section of the Great Pyramid against the sky, apparently intended to demonstrate the perfect orientation of the monument's faces towards the four cardinal points. It draws our attention to the fact that the Descending Passage effectively pointed towards Alpha Draconis – the closest star to real north at the beginning of the 3rd millennium BC, due to the precession of the equinoxes. This was the route connecting the dead king with the circumpolar stars, which never disappeared beneath the horizon and were therefore synonymous with eternity.

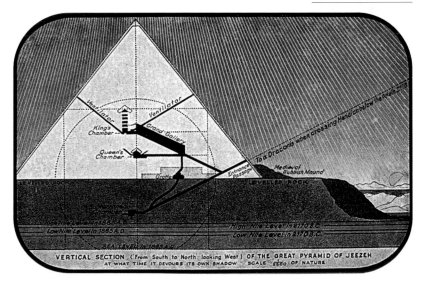

VERTICAL SECTION (From South to North looking West) OF THE GREAT PYRAMID OF JEEZEH
AT WHAT TIME IT DEVOURS ITS OWN SHADOW   SCALE 1/600 OF NATURE

whose author champions the 'biblical' theories. The gist of Davidson's message is clear from his title: he believes that concealed within the Great Pyramid's precise measurements are prophetic dates just waiting to be uncovered by the initiated. Spencer Lewis, author of *The Symbolic Prophecy of the Great Pyramid*, published in 1936, was another 'fanatic' and contemporary of Erman, as was Georges Barbarin, whose *Le Secret de la Grande Pyramide ou la Fin du monde adamique*, published the same year and running to several editions, took up Davidson's theories. We have to smile when we hear that the Great Pyramid, described as the world's first astronomer and first geometrician, carries in its fabric the mark of a superhuman knowledge, or when we read of precise dates recorded in the stone. We might also mention Helena P. Blavatsky and her *Isis Unveiled*, which, at the end of the 19th century, sought to demonstrate that the interior of Khufu's pyramid was a majestic temple where the royal family underwent initiation rites, the pharaoh's sarcophagus becoming, in Blavatsky's version of things, the font. Closer to our own time, we have Adam Rutherford and his *Pyramidology* (four volumes published between 1957 and 1972), for whom the Bible says in words what the Great Pyramid expresses in stone, and André Pochan explaining, in *L'Énigme de la Grande Pyramide* (1971), that if Khufu's pyramid is indeed a tomb, it is also a place of cultic initiation into the rites of Isis.

Opposite: For Barbarin, inspired by Davidson, the succession of routes leading to the King's Chamber are a material expression of the passage of time. On this section, junctions and changes in the angle of slope supposedly correspond to important dates, such as those of the Exodus or the birth of Christ.

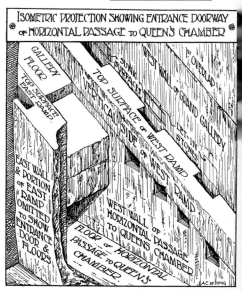

Above: Davidson's book on the Great Pyramid is nearly 600 pages long and full of dozens of tables and foldouts littered with numbers and dates, giving it the appearance of a work of serious scholarship, it is actually pseudo-science.

Unanswered Questions

We can only deduce for ourselves – from the small range of possibilities – how the pyramids were actually constructed, since the ancient Egyptians tell us nothing. The last ten years have seen almost as many 'definitive'

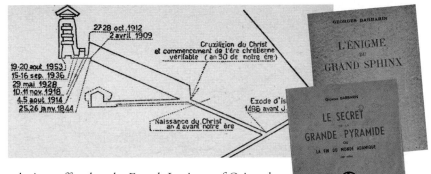

solutions offered to the French Institute of Oriental Archaeology in Cairo. What is certain is that the pyramids exist, overwhelmingly, and that they were built by human hands. That, one way or another, human beings succeeded in raising these prodigious mounds of stone, some of whose slabs, situated at the heart of the monument, tens of metres above the ground, weigh as much as 60 tons.

There are essentially two schools of thought, based on the evidence provided by Herodotus and Diodorus Siculus. There are those who think that the pyramids were built using some kind of lifting equipment – a type of crane or 'rocking hoist' based on the shadoof, consisting of a pivot and a counterweight and used for raising water – and those who maintain that ramps were needed, two approaches that are not necessarily incompatible. The remains of ramps have in fact been found at Giza itself and at other sites such as Meidum, Abu Ghurob and Lisht – proof that they did exist – and it is hard to see how the ancient builders could have managed without them. What is not quite certain is what form these ramps took, depending on whether they were used to bring slabs from nearby quarries or from the quays where stones from further afield were unloaded – granite from Aswan, for example, and limestone from Turah – or to lay successive courses during the actual construction of the

Above: The King's Chamber plays an important part in the Great Pyramid's so-called 'mysteries'. In the 19th century, the theosophist Helena P. Blavatsky claimed that Khufu's stone sarcophagus was used as a font. Whether it was actually used or not, Khufu's sarcophagus was only ever intended to serve as a receptacle for the dead king's body.

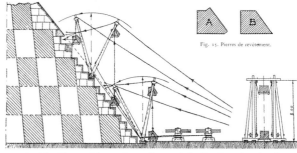

Fig. 15. Pierres de revêtement.

Left: In the 1950s, H. Strub-Roessler put forward a theory of how the casing of the great pyramids was built. He came up with a system starting at the top of the pyramids and working downwards using a series of derricks. It assumed the existence of bevelled slabs (A) but has since been shown to be wrong: examination of the casing slabs still in place at the top of Khafre's pyramid (B) shows they were laid starting at the bottom and working upwards, and later dressed working from the top down.

pyramid. Alongside various frontal, helical and mixed-type ramps, the latest hypothesis, put forward by Jean-Pierre and Henri Houdin, relates to an 'interior' spiral ramp, beginning at the level of the sixth course of masonry.

A number of other ideas have also been proposed, with surprisingly little basis in reality. Manuel Minguez, for example, a civil engineer unfamiliar with the topography of the Giza site, suggests the existence of a series of locks. Joseph Davidovits and (despite his readiness to explain the astonishing way that some of the slabs are fitted) Joël Bertho both reckon that Khufu's pyramid is made of slabs of 'reconstituted' stone. The American medium Edgar Cayce gave hundreds of 'readings' between 1901 and 1944 explaining that the Great Pyramid was built in 10,500 BC by survivors from Atlantis who needed neither ramps nor machines, since they were able to make the stone slabs 'float' at will!

Modern Technology at the Great Pyramid

Since the end of the 1980s, a wide range of modern techniques have been brought to bear on the Great Pyramid with the aim of probing and exploring specific areas and testing out a number of hypotheses.

In 1986, geophysical measurements recorded by the Egyptian Antiquities

Organization (EAO) as part of a study undertaken by the two French architects Gilles Dormion and Jean-Patrice Goidin detected an 'absence of mass' behind the west wall of the horizontal passage leading to the Queen's Chamber. Three holes were drilled at the base of this wall, which is unusual in that not all of its courses are made up of overlapping slabs, and revealed the presence of a fine sand, a discovery that was more significant than appeared at the time. The following year, a Japanese team from Waseda University in Tokyo, led by Sakuji Yoshimura, produced even more precise measurements and confirmed the same anomalies. Meanwhile, the EAO undertook a microgravimetric study of the pyramid which demonstrated varying densities 'such as would be expected from the presence of an internal stepped structure'.

Between 1990 and 1995, the Frenchman Jean Kerisel set about investigating Herodotus's claim that Khufu effectively sited his tomb on an island by having a series of subterranean chambers hollowed out of the bedrock and diverting water from the river via an underground channel. Kerisel was able to work in the King's Chamber,

The frontal ramp system suggested by J.-P. Lauer (opposite, centre) presupposes a volume of materials comparable to that of the pyramid under construction. Other possible solutions have been put forward (opposite, below), including an internal ramp, a 3D model of which (by Jean-Pierre Houdin) is shown below. Whatever form it took, the ramp must have had a sufficiently gentle gradient to allow for the haulage of vast slabs of stone, some of them weighing over 50 tons. The most likely solution seems to be a lateral ramp which wrapped around the entire pyramid.

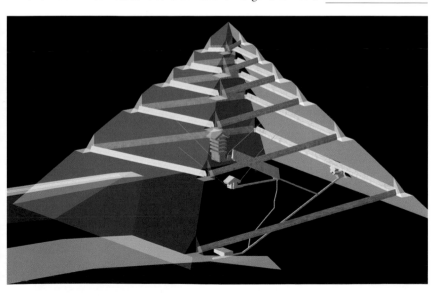

then later the Subterranean Chamber, where he received permission to use radar and even to drill into the bedrock floor, but he found nothing to substantiate the Greek historian's assertions.

In 1992, under the aegis of the German Archaeological Institute in Cairo, Rudolf Gantenbrink explored the 'air shafts' leading off the King's Chamber using a camera mounted on a small robot, which he had designed himself and named Upuaut after the Egyptian god responsible for 'opening up' paths. He repeated the exercise the following year, with Upuaut II, in the southern shaft of the Queen's Chamber: the robot crawled 65 metres up a 45° slope, but the shaft was blocked by a stone grandiosely described as a 'door', with two copper pins fixed in it. In 2002, Zahi Hawass repeated the experiment with a new robot, Pyramid Rover. He explored both the air shafts leading from the Queen's Chamber and drilled a hole in the limestone slab blocking the southern one so that an optical fibre could be inserted. Media interest was high, but the results were disappointing: there was no 'secret chamber', simply a small cavity – and another stone slab.

Below: Apart from the removal of its casing, Khufu's pyramid has sustained no external damage – unlike Menkaure's pyramid, which has a breach in its northern face – so that its core structure remains concealed. In 1987, variations in density were recorded using microgravimetry: the results appear to reveal the existence of concentric steps rather than a possible 'spiral' structure.

DENSITY
- \> 2.30
- 2.05–2.30
- 1.95–2.05
- 1.85–1.95
- < 1.85

An Increasingly Likely Hypothesis

There have been many recent studies of the pyramids using sophisticated technical resources, but one that really stands out is Gilles Dormion's, as described in his book *La Chambre de Chéops*, published in 2004.

Dormion knows Khufu's pyramid intimately, having produced the most precise survey of it, and he and Jean-Yves Verd'hurt have come to the conclusion that, although the King's Chamber was intended to serve as the pharaoh's eternal resting place,

the body may actually never have been placed there. Far from fantasizing about hypothetical hidden treasure, the two Frenchmen have merely made a number of commonplace observations and drawn the relevant conclusions. It is clear, for a start, that this part of the pyramid structure was badly compromised after the five stress-relieving chambers were built: 2,500 tons of granite were used to form these chambers, and the sheer weight of them has compressed the limestone ashlar beneath the chamber's southern wall and broken its nine roof beams. Their undersides are cracked at the southern end of the chamber, and the beams show signs of having been shored up at both their southern and northern ends: those who were responsible for these repairs knew, therefore, that the beams were also cracked at their northern end, but to ascertain this they would have needed to make an inspection of the first relieving chamber.

Other than the pyramid builders, who could actually have known that there was a cavity above the royal burial vault? Who else could have known the exact level of this cavity, and that to access it they needed to excavate a narrow passage first in an easterly, then in a southerly direction – the same passage whose mouth Davison discovered in 1765 in the Grand Gallery's topmost course?

Given all this, it would be natural to suppose that a funerary apartment originally abandoned due to a change of plan might have been re-used in order to avoid burying Khufu in a chamber that was in danger of

Above: The robot Pyramid Rover, equipped with a camera, was used in 2002 to explore the air shafts leading from the Queen's Chamber. The idea was to measure the length of the shafts, but also to determine whether they led to more chambers, whose existence nevertheless seemed unlikely since they would have been located only 10 metres or so from the pyramid's exterior faces. The shafts, discovered by an English engineer, Waynman Dixon, in 1872, are narrow (about 20 cm wide) and nothing like them has been found in any other pyramid. Their function is almost certainly technical rather than symbolic: dug as an open channel on the side of a slab, and sealed by movable plugs, they would have served to ensure that no shearing occurred between courses of masonry.

imminent collapse. This must seem especially likely as the risk appears to have influenced the pyramid architects to the point that no chamber of any sort would ever again be located within the superstructure of a pyramid. Since Khufu's Subterranean Chamber was never finished, we can see by glancing at a cross-section of his pyramid that the only possible location for the new burial vault was in the vicinity of the Queen's Chamber, which might merely have served as an antechamber.

PLAN

There are also a number of unusual features to this chamber, and more often than not these have been incorrectly interpreted – in particular, the corbelled niche in the east wall, which cannot have been intended for a statue, as has been supposed. Geophysical measurements were needed if we were to learn more. Permission to use georadar was granted, and Jean-Pierre Baron, a geophysicist with the French company SAFEGE, came to take the necessary measurements in the autumn of 2000.

Analysis of his results looks very promising. It appears that there is a passage two cubits wide beneath the Queen's Chamber and that this passage, coming from the east, leads into the heart of the pyramid, at the exact intersection of the east–west and north–south axes. The use of an optical fibre (as was used to demonstrate the existence of the 'relieving chambers' in the Meidum pyramid) would clearly be sufficient to verify the existence of this passage – and that of a possible, as yet undiscovered chamber.

It is worth adding, as a final point, that measurements taken in the autumn of 2000 using microgravimetry and geo-radar have demonstrated a density loss in Khafre's pyramid too, probably due to the presence of a 'cavity of

Above: All the north–south radar maps produced on the floor of the Queen's Chamber present the same echo pattern, indicating the presence of a structure approximately a metre wide, orientated in an east–west direction, whose roof is about 3.5 metres below floor level.

some size and significance', and intermittent anomalies which could correspond to the access to this cavity.

It seems that the Giza Pyramids have not told us everything yet, and the myths associated more specifically with Khufu's continue to flourish.

Below: A number of features suggest the importance of the niche let into the east wall of the Queen's Chamber. Its position, off-set from the centre axis of the chamber, its corbelled sides (pointless in a statue niche), and the fact that the sap dug by looters in the second course of masonry is in

fact a continuation of a properly constructed shaft all indicate that it was an essential structural element.

DOCUMENTS

The Pyramids Seen by the Ancients

The earliest surviving writings on the pyramids come from Greek and Roman authors. In the 5th century BC, Herodotus explained the construction of the pyramids in great detail. Following him, Diodorus Siculus was astonished by the architectural skill that they displayed, while Pliny the Elder criticized them as the 'idle and frivolous' follies of ostentatious monarchs.

Machines to Build the Pyramids

I was also informed by the same priests that, till the reign of Rhampsinitus, Egypt was not only remarkable for its abundance, but for its excellent laws. Cheops, who succeeded this prince, degenerated into the extremest profligacy of conduct. He barred the avenues to every temple, and forbade the Egyptians to offer sacrifices. He proceeded next to make them labour servilely for himself. Some he compelled to hew stones in the quarries of the Arabian mountains, and drag them to the banks of the Nile; others were appointed to receive them in vessels, and transport them to a mountain of Libya. For this service a hundred thousand men were employed, who were relieved every three months. Ten years were consumed in the hard labour of forming the road through which these stones were to be drawn; a work, in my estimation, of no less fatigue and difficulty than the pyramid itself. This causeway is five stadia in length, forty cubits wide, and its extreme height thirty-two cubits, the whole is of polished marble, adorned with the figures of animals. Ten years, as I remarked, were exhausted in forming this causeway, not to mention the time employed in the vaults of the hill upon which the pyramids are erected. These he intended as a place of burial for himself, and were in an island which he formed by introducing the waters of the Nile. The pyramid itself was a work of twenty years. It is of a square form; every front is eight plethora long, and as many in height; the stones very skilfully cemented, and none of them of less dimensions than thirty feet.

The ascent of the pyramid was regularly graduated by what some call steps, and others altars. Having finished the first flight, they elevated the stones to the second by the aid of machines constructed of short pieces of wood; from the second, by a similar engine, they were raised to the third, and so on to the summit. Thus there were as many machines as there were regular divisions in the ascent of the pyramid, though in fact there might only be one, which, being easily manageable, might be removed from one range of the building to another as often as occasion made it necessary. Both modes have been told me, and I know not which best deserves credit. The summit of the pyramid was first of all finished; descending thence, they regularly completed the whole. Upon the outside were inscribed, in Egyptian characters, the various sums of money expended, in the progress of the work, for the radishes, onions, and garlic consumed by the artificers. This, as I well remember, my interpreter informed me, amounted to no less a sum than one thousand six hundred talents. If this be true, how much more must it have necessarily cost for iron tools, food, and clothes for the workmen, particularly when we consider the length of time they were employed on the building itself, adding what was spent in the hewing and conveyance of the stones, and the construction of the subterranean apartments?

Cheops having exhausted his wealth, was so flagitious, that he degraded his daughter, commanding her to make the most of her opportunities. She complied with her father's injunctions, but I was not told what sum she thus procured: at the same time she took care to perpetuate the memory of herself; with which view she solicited every one of her lovers to present her with a stone. With these it is reported the middle of the three pyramids, fronting the larger one, was constructed, the elevation of which on each side is one hundred and fifty feet.

According to the Egyptians, this Cheops reigned fifty years. His brother Chephren succeeded to his throne, and adopted a similar conduct. He also built a pyramid, but this was less than his brother's, for I measured them both; it has no subterraneous chambers, nor any channel for the admission of the Nile, which in the other pyramid surrounds an island, where the body of Cheops is said to be deposited. Of this

latter pyramid, the first ascent is entirely of Ethiopian marble of divers colours, but it is not so high as the larger pyramid, near which it stands, by forty feet. This Chephren reigned fifty-six years; the pyramid he built stands on the same hill with that erected by his brother: the hill itself is near one hundred feet high.

Herodotus,
Egypt and Scythia Described by Herodotus, London, Paris, New York & Melbourne: Cassell & Company Ltd, 1886

Wonder and Astonishment

Chemmis, the eighth king from Remphis, was of Memphis, and reigned fifty years. He built the greatest of the three pyramids, which were accounted amongst the seven wonders of the world. They stand towards Libya, one hundred and twenty furlongs from Memphis, and forty-five from the Nile. The greatness of these works, and the excessive labour of the workmen seen in them, do even strike the beholders with admiration and astonishment. The greatest being four-square, took up, on every square, seven hundred feet of ground in the basis, and above six hundred feet in height, spiring up narrower by little and little, till it came up to the point, the top of which was six cubits square. It is built of solid marble throughout, of rough work, but of perpetual duration: for though it be now a thousand years since it was built, (some say above three thousand and four hundred), yet the stones are as firmly jointed, and the whole building as entire and without the least decay, as they were at the first laying an erection. The stone, they say, was brought a long way off, out of Arabia, and that the work was raised by making mounts of earth; cranes and other engines being not known at that time. And that which is most to be admired, is to see such a foundation so imprudently laid, as it seems to be, in a sandy place, where there is not the least sign of any earth cast up, nor marks where any stone was cut and polished; so that the whole pile seems to be reared all at once, and fixed in the midst of heaps of sand by some god, and not built by degrees by the hands of men. Some of the Egyptians tell wonderful things, and invent strange fables concerning these works, affirming that the mounts were made of salt and salt-petre, and that they were melted by the inundation of the river, and being so dissolved, every thing was washed away but the building itself. But this is not the truth of the thing; but the great multitude of hands that raised the mounts, the same carried back the earth to the place whence they dug it; for they say, there were three hundred and sixty thousand men employed in this work, and the whole was scarce completed in twenty years time.

When this king was dead, his brother Cephres succeeded him, and reigned six-and-fifty years: some say it was not his brother, but his son Chabryis that came to the crown: but all agree in this, that the successor, in imitation of his predecessor, erected another pyramid like to the former, both in structure and artificial workmanship, but not near so large, every square of the basis being only a furlong in breadth. Upon the greater pyramid was inscribed the value of the herbs and onions that were spent upon the labourers during the works, which amounted to above sixteen hundred talents.

There is nothing written upon the lesser: the entrance and ascent is only on one side, cut by steps into the main stone. Although the kings designed these two for their sepulchres, yet it happened that neither of them were there buried. For the people, being incensed at them by the reason of the toil and labour they were put to, and the cruelty and oppression of their kings, threatened to drag their carcases out of their graves, and pull them by piece-meal, and cast them to the dogs; and therefore both of them upon their beds commanded their servants to bury them in some obscure place.

After him reigned Mycerinus, (otherwise called Cherinus), the son of him who built the first pyramid. This prince began a third, but died before it was finished; every square of the basis was three hundred feet. The walls for fifteen stories high were of black marble, like that of Thebes, the rest was of the same stone with the other pyramids. Though the other pyramids went beyond this in greatness, yet this far excelled the rest in the curiosity of the structure, and the largeness of the stones. On that side of the pyramid towards the north, was inscribed the name of the founder Mycerinus. This king, they say, detesting the severity of the former kings, carried himself all his days gently and graciously towards all his subjects, and did all that possibly he could to gain their love and good will towards him; besides other things, he expended vast sums of money upon the oracles and worship of the gods; and bestowing large gifts upon honest men, whom he judged to be injured, and to be hardly dealt with in the courts of justice.

There are other pyramids, every square of which are two hundred feet in the basis; and in all things like unto the others, except in bigness. It is said that these three last kings built them for their wives.

It is not in the least to be doubted, but that these pyramids far excel all the other works throughout Egypt, not only in the greatness and costs of the building, but in the excellency of the workmanship: for the architects, (they say), are much more to be admired than the kings themselves that were at the cost. For those performed all by their own ingenuity, but these did nothing but by the wealth handed to them by descent from their predecessors, and by the toil and labour of other men.

Diodorus Siculus, *Historical Library of Diodorus the Sicilian,* Vol. 1, translated by G. Booth, London: Davis, 1814

Monuments to Vanity

We must make some mention, too, however cursorily, of the Pyramids of Egypt, so many idle and frivolous pieces of ostentation of their resources, on the part of the monarchs of that country. Indeed, it is asserted by most persons, that the only motive for constructing them, was either a determination not to leave their treasures to their successors or to rivals that might be plotting to supplant them, or to prevent the lower classes from remaining unoccupied. There was great vanity displayed by these men in constructions of this description, and there are still the remains of many of them in an unfinished state. There is one to be seen in the Nome of Arsinoïtes; two in that of Memphites, not far from the Labyrinth, of which we shall shortly have to speak; and two in the place where Lake Moeris was excavated, an immense artificial piece of water, cited by the Egyptians among their wondrous and memorable works: the summits of the pyramids, it is said, are to be seen above the water.

The other three pyramids, the renown of which has filled the whole earth, and which are conspicuous from every quarter to persons navigating the river, are situated on the African side of it, upon a rocky sterile elevation. They lie between the city of Memphis and what we have mentioned as the Delta, within four miles of the river, and seven miles and a-half from Memphis, near a village known as Busiris, the people of which are in the habit of ascending them.

In front of these pyramids is the Sphinx, a still more wondrous object of art, but one upon which silence has been observed, as it is looked upon as a divinity by the people of the neighbourhood. It is their belief that King Harmaïs was buried in it, and they will have it that it was brought there from a distance. The truth is, however, that it was hewn from the solid rock; and, from a feeling of veneration, the face of the monster is coloured red....

The largest Pyramid is built of stone quarried in Arabia: three hundred and sixty thousand men, it is said, were employed upon it twenty years, and the three were completed in seventy-eight years and four months. They are described by the following writers: Herodotus, Euhemerus, Duris of Samos, Aristagoras, Dionysius, Artemidorus, Alexander Polyhistor, Butoridas, Antisthenes, Demetrius, Demoteles, and Apion. These authors, however, are disagreed as to the persons by whom they were constructed; accident having, with very considerable justice, consigned to oblivion the names of those who erected such stupendous memorials of their vanity. Some of these writers inform us that fifteen hundred talents were expended upon radishes, garlic, and onions alone.

The largest Pyramid occupies seven jugera of ground, and the four angles are equidistant, the face of each side being eight hundred and thirty-three feet in length. The total height from the ground to the summit is seven hundred and twenty-five feet, and the platform on the summit is sixteen feet and a-half in circuit. Of the second Pyramid, the faces of the four sides are each seven hundred and fifty-seven feet and a-half in length. The third is smaller than the others, but far more prepossessing in appearance: it is built of Ethiopian stone, and the face between the four corners is three hundred and sixty-three feet in extent. In the vicinity of these erections, there are no vestiges of any buildings left. Far and wide there is nothing but sand to be seen, of a grain somewhat like a lentil in appearance, similar to that of the greater part of Africa, in fact.

The most difficult problem is to know how the materials for construction could possibly be carried to so vast a height. According to some authorities, as the building gradually advanced, they heaped up against it vast mounds of nitre and salt; which piles were melted after its completion, by introducing beneath them the waters of the river. Others, again, maintain, that bridges were constructed, of bricks of clay, and that, when the pyramid was completed, these bricks were distributed for erecting the houses of private individuals. For the level of the river, they say, being so much lower, water could never by any possibility have been brought there by the medium of canals. In the interior of the largest Pyramid there is a well, eighty-six cubits deep, which communicates with the river, it is thought. The method of ascertaining the height of the Pyramids and all similar edifices was discovered by Thales of Miletus; he measuring the shadow at the hour of the day at which it is equal in length to the body projecting it.

Such are the marvellous Pyramids; but the crowning marvel of all is, that the smallest, but most admired of them – that we may feel no surprise at the opulence of the kings – was built by Rhodopis, a courtesan! This woman was once the fellow-slave of Aesopus the philosopher and fabulist, and the sharer of his bed; but what is much more surprising is that a courtesan should have been enabled, by her vocation, to amass such enormous wealth.

Pliny the Elder, *The Natural History* (eds. John Bostock and H. T. Riley), Book XXXVI, Chapters 16–17, London: Taylor and Francis, 1855

An Arabic Perspective

The Arabic literature that flourished between the tenth and the fifteenth centuries AD is full of the admiration of its authors for the architectural prowess and construction skills of the builders of the ancient pyramids. They became the subject of many legends and stories, as well as factual accounts, such as this one by famed physician and traveller Abd-al-Latif, taken from his vivid and detailed Account of Egypt.

Of all the countries I have seen for myself, or know through the accounts of others, there is not one that can compare with Egypt in terms of the great number of ancient monuments to be found there.

The pyramids are one of the wonders of that country: they have attracted the attention of a very great number of writers, who have described these edifices in their works and recorded their dimensions. There are a very large number of them, and they are all situated on the same side of the river as Giza, in line with Egypt's ancient capital, and in an area that can be covered on foot in roughly two days. […] There are both large pyramids and small ones; some are constructed of mud and bricks, but the majority are built of stone. There are those that are made up of steps or tiers; but the greatest number are precisely pyramidal in shape and have smooth surfaces.

[…] With reference now to those pyramids that have formed the object of so many accounts, that we distinguish from all the rest, and admire above all for their size, they are three in number, aligned at Giza, opposite Fostat, located a short distance from one another, and angled in the direction of the rising sun. Two out of these three pyramids are enormous. The poets who have described them have given way to all the fervour which these monuments inspired in them; they have compared them to two immense breasts rising from the bosom of Egypt. They are very close to each other, and are built of white stones; the third, which lacks a quarter of the size of the other two, is constructed of red granite that is speckled in appearance and extremely hard. Iron makes barely any impression upon it. This pyramid seems small when compared with the other two; but when one draws close and it fills one's vision, the effect is almost stupefying, and gazing upon it tires the eyes.

We are bound to admire the form, and the solidity, of the pyramids' construction: it is to this form that they owe their success in resisting the efforts of the centuries, or we might say rather that time itself has resisted the efforts of these eternal edifices. Indeed, when we reflect deeply on the construction of the pyramids, we are forced to recognize that the greatest geniuses have lavished their most cunning designs upon it and the keenest minds have devoted all their ingenuity to it. [...]

What is truly remarkable about these edifices is the pyramid shape adopted in their construction, starting from a square base and finishing with a point. One of the properties of this shape is that the centre of gravity lies at the very heart of the edifice, with the result that it leans upon itself and supports the weight of its own mass, that all its parts bear respectively upon one another, and that it does not gravitate towards a point outside itself.

[...] One of these pyramids is open and has an entrance allowing access to the interior. This opening leads to a series of narrow passages, to shafts extending downwards to a great depth, and to wells and precipices, as confirmed by those who are bold enough to climb down there; for there are a great many people who are drawn in by their fanciful hopes and by a foolish cupidity. They descend into the deepest recesses of the edifice until they reach a place beyond which they can proceed no further. The customary, and most frequently used, route is a glacis leading towards the upper part of the pyramid, where a square chamber is to be found, with a stone sarcophagus inside it.

The opening giving access to the interior today is not the door that was built at the time of the pyramid's construction, but a hole that was dug at random and required some effort to make. We are told that it was made at the behest of the Caliph Mamun. The majority of our company entered by this route and climbed up to the chamber at the top of the pyramid. When they came down, they recounted the wonderful things they had seen, and reported that this passage was so full of bats and bat

droppings as to be all but blocked; that the bats were almost as big as pigeons, and that in the upper part there were windows and openings that seemed to have been constructed in order to allow in light and air. [...]

These pyramids are built of large stones, ten to twenty cubits long, two to three cubits thick and the same wide. What is particularly admirable is the extreme precision with which these stones have been bonded and arranged one on top of the other. Their courses are so carefully aligned that it would be impossible to thread a needle or a hair between two of these stones. They are bound together by a mortar that forms a layer as thin as a sheet of paper: I have never encountered such mortar before and do not know what it is made of. The stones are covered with writing in those ancient characters which we are no longer able to decipher today. I have never met anyone in the whole of Egypt who was able to say that they knew, even by hearsay, anyone who could read those characters. There are so many of these inscriptions that, if we wanted to copy on paper only those that we see on the surface of these two pyramids, we would fill more than ten thousand pages.

I have read in certain books by the ancient Sabaeans that one of these two pyramids is the tomb of Agathodemon and the other the tomb of Hermes. According to them, they are two great prophets. [...] They say that people made pilgrimages to these two pyramids from every country in the world.

Abd al-Latif, *Account of Egypt*, late 12th–early 13th century

Travellers from the West

Even before the Egyptian expedition of 1798, many Western travellers had written accounts of their visits to the Pyramids of Giza, telling of perilous ascents to the high summit or tense excursions inside the Great Pyramid. In the 17th century, Georges Sandys called them 'too great a morsel for time to devour'. By the 19th century, while Vivant Denon produced an awed description of the Sphinx, Chateaubriand saw the pyramids as an 'everlasting gate erected on the confines of eternity.'

'Chief of the World's Seven Wonders'

Full West of the City, close upon those Desarts, aloft on a rocky level adjoining to the Valley, stand those three Pyramides (the barbarous Monuments of prodigality and vain-glory) so universally celebrated. The name is derived from a flame of fire in regard of their shape, broad below, and sharp above, like a pointed Diamond. By such the Ancient did express the original of things; and that formless form-taking substance. For as a Pyramis beginning at a point, and the principal height by little and little dilateth into all parts: so Nature proceeding from one undivideable Fountain (even God the Soveraign Essence) receiveth diversity of Forms; effused into several kinds and multitudes of Figures; uniting all in the Supreme head, from whence all excellencies issue. The labours of the *Jews*, as themselves report, and is alledged by *Josephus*, were employed in these; which deserveth little better credit (for what they built was of Brick) than that absurd opinion of *Naziazenzus*; who, out of the consonancy of the names, affirmeth, that they were built by *Joseph* for Granaries, against the seven years of Famine; when as one was thrice seven years, saving one, in erecting. But by the testimony of all that have writ, amongst whom *Lucan*,

When high Pyramides do grace
The Ghosts of Ptolomies lewd race:

and by what shall be said hereafter, most manifest it is that these, as the rest, were the regal Sepulchres of the *Egyptians*. The greatest of the three, and chief of the world's seven wonders, being square at the bottom, is supposed to take up eight Acres of ground. Every square being 300 single paces in length, the square at the top, consisting of three Stones only, yet large enough for threescore to stand upon, ascended by two hundred fifty five steps, each step above three feet high, of a breadth proportionable. No Stone so little throughout the whole, as to be drawn by our Carriages: yet were these hewn out of the *Trojan* Mountains far off in *Arabia*; so called of Captive *Trojans* brought by *Menalaus* unto *Egypt*, and there afterward planted. A wonder how conveyed hither: how so mounted, a greater. Twenty years was it building; by three hundred threescore and six thousand men continually wrought upon: who only in Radishes, Garlick, and Onions, are said to have consumed one thousand and eight hundred Talents. By these and the like inventions exhausted by their Treasure, and employed the people; for fear lest such infinite wealth should corrupt their Successors, and dangerous idleness beget in the Subject a desire of innovation. Besides, they considering the frailty of man, that in an instant buds, blows, and withereth; did endeavour by such sumptuous and magnificent Structures, in spite of death to give unto their fames eternity. But vainly:

Not sumptuous Pyramids to Skies up-rear'd,
Nor Elean Joves proud Fane, which
Heaven compeer'd,
Nor the right fortune of Maufolus Tomb,
Are priviledg'd from deaths extremest doom:
Or fire, or worms, their glories do abate,
Or they, age-shaken, fall with their own
weight.

Yet this hath been too great a morsel for time to devour; having stood, as may be probably conjectured, about three thousand and two hundred years: and now rather old than ruinous: yet the North-side is most worn, by reason of the humidity of the Northern wind, which is here the moistest. The top at length we ascended, with many pauses and much difficulty; from whence, with delighted eyes, we beheld that Soveraign

of Streams, and most excellent of Countries. South-ward and near hand the *Mummes*: afar off divers huge Pyramides; each of which, were this away, might supply the repute of a wonder.

George Sandys, *Sandys Travels*,
London: John Williams Junior, 1673

'Heaps of Wrought Stone Placed in Form of a Pyramid'

Our next Digression was to the famous Pyramids of *Egypt*, which stand about six or seven Miles from *Cairo*, at the Entrance of the Desarts of Africa, and are usually reckon'd amongst the Seven Wonders of the World, and the only one of the Seven that is now standing, the Walls of *Babylon* being long since demolish'd, the Temple of *Diana* burnt, the Statue of *Jupiter Olympicus* and *Colossus* of *Rhodes* broken in pieces, the *Mausolaeum* of *Artemisia* and *Labyrinth* of *Daedalus* utterly ruin'd, and nothing but their name remaining. Not to mention divers smaller Pyramids that are dispersed up and down the Desarts, we shall only insist on the three most remarkable. They are nothing but prodigious Heaps of wrought Stone placed in form of a Pyramid, erected on a square Base, and lessening by degrees to the very top. The greatest and fairest of the three has about Three hundred and twenty two of my paces on each side at the Base, so that the whole compass must be of One thousand two hundred ninety two paces: But it's so cover'd with heaps of Sand, thrown up by the Wind, that 'tis impossible to take the just measures; and, indeed, two of the opposite sides seem, to the Eye, to be larger than the other two; so that the Base must be oblong. Its Height seems to be equal to one side of the Base. It has Steps all round, on the out-side, in form of an *Amphitheatre*, by which we ascended, tho' not without some difficulty and danger, the Stones being narrow, and in some places so worn, that we had much ado to get up. At mid-way we found a place made expresly, as we imagin'd, for People to repose, it being capable of nine or ten Persons. Having rested a while, we proceeded on to the top, which, though it seems to terminate in a point, to such as view it from below, can nevertheless contain forty Persons very commodiously. From thence we had a Prospect on one side of the barren sandy Desarts of *Africa*; and on the other *Cairo*, the *Nile*, and all the adjoyning Country, with all the Towns and Villages, to our great satisfaction. The other two Pyramids terminate in a point, and hence 'tis conjectur'd, that there might have been some Colossus erected on this; and, indeed, we observ'd an hollow place in which some Statue seems to have been fasten'd; but there is nothing to be seen at present but the names of such People as have been there cut out on the Stones. Having made our Collation with such Provisions as we could conveniently carry up, and being half broil'd by the excessive Heat of the Sun, we descended the same way, but with far greater hazard than when we came up; as well by reason of the bad Way, as the Terrour with which the Precipice struck us, where we must have inevitably perish'd if we had miss'd our footing: But, God be prais'd, we got safely to the bottom. It has Two hundred and six Steps, the lowermost being so very high that a Man has much ado to get up, but the rest decrease gradually to the top. We also visited its in-side, and entring with lighted Torches, were forced to creep on our Hands and Knees to the middle of the Pyramid, where we found

an hollow Passage, like a large Chimney, running from the bottom almost to the top, with holes cut out on both sides to fasten one's Feet in as he ascends. Having got to a considerable height, we found a pretty little Chamber, adorn'd with Marble, with a Tomb at the further end, said to be the *Pharaoh*'s, where he design'd to have been buried, had he not left his Carcass in the *Red Sea*, pursuing the Children of *Israel* when they left *Egypt*. Near this Chamber we saw another much like the former; but finding nothing more that deserv'd our Curiosity, we return'd by the same way. The other two Pyramids are much lesser than this, without any Ascent, and of no great Note.

Ellis Veryard, *An Account of Divers Choice Remarks…Taken in a Journey through the Low Countries …*, London, 1701

'A Useless Sepulchre'

Destructive time, and the still more destructive hand of man, which have so defaced and destroyed all the other monuments of antiquity, have hitherto been able to effect but little against the pyramids. The solidity of their construction, and their enormous size, have secured them against every attempt, and seem to promise them an eternal duration. All travellers speak of them with enthusiasm, and enthusiasm they may well inspire. These artificial mountains are first discovered at ten leagues distance. They seem to retire in proportion as they are approached; and when still a league off, tower with such loftiness above our heads, that we imagine ourselves at their feet; but when at length we reach them, nothing can express the various sensations they inspire. Their stupendous height, the steep declivity of their sides, their prodigious surface, their enormous solidity, the distant ages they recall to memory, the recollection of the labour they must have cost, and the reflection that these huge rocks are the work of man, so diminutive and feeble, who crawls at their feet, lost in wonder, awe, humiliation, and reverence, altogether impress the mind of the spectator in a manner not to be described; but to this first transport other sentiments soon succeed. Elevated as we are with so exalted a proof of the power of man, when we consider the purpose for which these amazing works were intended, we cannot but view them with regret. We lament, that to construct a useless sepulchre, a whole nation should have been rendered miserable for twenty years: we groan over the numberless acts of injustice and oppression these tiresome labours must have cost, in conveying, preparing, and piling up such an immense mass of stones; and we are inflamed with indignation at the tyranny of the despots who enforced these barbarous works, a sentiment indeed which too frequently recurs on viewing the different monuments of Egypt. Those labyrinths, temples, and pyramids, by their huge and heavy structure, attest much less the genius of a nation, opulent and friendly to the arts, than the fervitude of a people who were slaves to the caprices of their monarchs; and we are even inclined to pardon that avarice, which, by violating their tombs, has frustrated their idle hopes: we bestow less pity on these ruins; and while the lover of the arts beholds with indignation, at Alexandria, the columns of her palaces sawed into *mill-stones*, the philosopher, after the first emotion, occasioned by the destruction of every fine work, cannot suppress a smile at the secret justice of that destiny, which restores to the people what cost them so much fruitless toil, and which renders the pride of unprofitable luxury subservient to the meanest of necessities.

The happiness of the people, rather than the preservation of the ancient monuments of Egypt, should certainly dictate the wish of seeing that country under the government of another nation; but were it only in the latter point of view, such a revolution would still be very desirable. Were Egypt possessed by a nation friendly to the fine arts, discoveries might be made there, which would make us better acquainted with antiquity than any thing the rest of the world can afford us. […] These countries, in which formerly were cities and temples, having never been subject to the devastations of the Barbarians, must have preserved their monuments, and the rather as it is probable they are but thinly inhabited, or perhaps entirely deserted; and these monuments, buried in the sands, must be preserved there, as a deposite for future generations. To a period less remote, possibly than we imagine, we must defer the gratification of our wishes and our hopes. We may then be allowed to search every part of the country, the banks of the Nile, and the sands of Libya. We may then be permitted to open the small pyramid of Djiza, the total demolition of which would not cost fifty thousand livres (two thousand pounds). It is probable too, that till that period, we must remain ignorant of the signification of the hieroglyphics; though, in my opinion, the means we at present possess may be sufficient to explain them.

Count Constantin François de Volney, *Travels Through Syria and Egypt*, London: 1787

'[The Sphinx] Seems Real Life and Flesh'

I had only time to view the sphinx, which deserves to be drawn with a most scrupulous attention, even more than has ever yet been bestowed upon it. Although its proportions are colossal, its outline is pure and graceful; the expression of the head is mild, gracious, and elegant; the character indeed is African; but the mouth, the lips of which are thick, has a softness and delicacy of execution truly admirable; it seems real life and flesh. Art must doubtless have been at a high degree of perfection when this monument was executed; for, if the head is defective in point of *style*, that is to say, the straight and bold lines which give expression to the figures under which the Greeks have designated their deities, yet sufficient justice has been rendered to the fine simplicity and character of Nature which is displayed in this figure.

Vivant Denon,
Travels in Upper and Lower Egypt,
translated by F. Blagdon,
London: James Ridgway, 1802

'The Entrance of a Life without End'

On leaving the canal of Menouf, and continuing to ascend the river, we perceived on our left the ridge of Mount Mokattam, and on our right the high sandy downs of Libya. In the intermediate space between these two chains of mountains, we soon descried the tops of the Pyramids, from which we were yet upwards of ten leagues distant. During the remainder of our voyage, which took us near eight hours, I remained upon deck to contemplate these tombs; which seemed to increase in magnitude and height as we approached. The Nile, which then resembled a little sea; the mixture of the sands of the desert, and the freshest verdure; the palm-trees, the sycamores, the domes, the mosques, and the minarets of Cairo; the distant pyramids of Sakkarah, from which the river seemed to issue as from its immense reservoirs, altogether formed a scene to which the world cannot produce a parallel. [...]

I confess, however, that at the first sight of the Pyramids, the only sentiment I felt was admiration. Philosophy, I know, can sigh or smile at the reflection that the most stupendous monument ever erected by the hand of man is a tomb: but why should we behold in the pyramid of Cheops nothing but a heap of stones and a skeleton? It was not from a sense of his nothingness that man reared such a sepulchre, but from the instinct of his immortality: this sepulchre is not the boundary that marks the termination of the career of a day, but the entrance of a life without end: 'tis an everlasting gate erected on the confines of eternity. "All these people" (of Egypt), says Diodorus Siculus, "considering the duration of life as a very short period, and of little importance, are on the other hand extremely solicitous about that long memory which virtue leaves behind it. For this reason they give to the habitations of the living the name of inns, where they sojourn only for a short time, but that of eternal abodes to the tombs of the dead, which they are never more to quit. Accordingly, the kings have manifested a certain indifference in regard to the construction of their palaces, and bestowed all their attention on that of their tombs."

It is insisted, at the present day, that all monuments had a physical utility, and it is not considered that there is a moral utility for nations of a much higher order, which was studied by the legislators of antiquity. Is, then, nothing to be learned from the sight of a tomb? If any lesson is taught by it, why should we complain that a king resolved to render that lesson perpetual? Majestic monuments constitute an essential part of the glory of every human society. Unless we maintain that it is a matter of indifference whether a nation leaves behind it a name or no name in history, we cannot condemn those structures which extend the memory of a people beyond its own existence, and make it contemporary with the future generations that fix their residence in its forsaken fields. Of what consequence is it then whether these edifices were amphitheatres or sepulchres? Every thing is a tomb with a nation that no longer exists. When man is gone, the monuments of his life are still more vain than those of his death: his mausoleum is at least serviceable to his ashes; but do his palaces retain any particle of his pleasures?

Most certainly, if we would be strict, a little grave is sufficient for all, and six feet of ground, as Matthew Molé observes, will always do justice to the greatest man in the world: God may be adored under a tree, as beneath the dome of St. Peter's; and a man may live in a cottage as well as in the Louvre. The error of this mode of reasoning consists in transferring one order of things in another. Besides, a nation is not more happy when it lives in ignorance of the arts, than when it leaves behind striking evidences of its genius. People have ceased to believe in the existence of those communities of shepherds who pass their days in innocence, and beguile the delicious hours with rambling in the recesses of forests. Full well we know that these honest pastors make war upon

each other, that they may feast upon the sheep of their neighbours. Their bowers are neither shaded with vines, nor embalmed with the perfume of flowers; you are suffocated in their habitations with the smoke, and stifled with the stench of milk. In poetry, and in philosophy, a petty, half-barbarous tribe may enjoy every earthly blessing; but merciless history subjects them to the same calamities as the rest of mankind. Are they who so loudly exclaim against glory—are they, I would ask, totally regardless of renown? For my part, so far from considering the monarch, who erected the great Pyramid, as a madman, I look upon him to have been a sovereign of a magnanimous disposition. The idea of vanquishing time by a tomb, of surviving generations, manners, laws, and ages, by a coffin, could not have sprung from a vulgar mind. If this be pride, it is at least a grand pride. Such a vanity as that which produced the great Pyramid, that has withstood the ravages of three or four thousand years, must certainly, in the end, be accounted as something.

Viscount François René de Chateaubriand, *Travels in Greece…*, translated by Frederic Shoberl, London: Henry Colburn, 1811

The Age of Discovery

In 1818, the Italian explorer Giovanni Battista Belzoni discovered the entrance to the pyramid of Khafre. This was just one of his achievements during a remarkable four-year period spent exploring major archaeological sites in Egypt, including Abu Simbel, Thebes and Karnak. On his return to Europe, he published an account of his travels and discoveries, from which the following extract is taken.

I was determined to proceed still farther with my researches, the recent disappointment making me rather more obstinate than I was before. I had given a day's rest to the Arabs, which I dedicated to a closer inspection of the pyramid. It often happens, that a man is so much ingulfed in the pursuit of his views, as to be in danger of losing himself, if he do not quickly find the means either of an honourable retreat, or of attaining the accomplishment of his intended purpose. Such was my case. The success of my discovery of the false passage was considered as a failure. I cared little what was thought of it, but I was provoked at having been deceived by those marks, which led me to the forced passage, with the loss of so much time and labour. However, I did not despair. I strictly noticed the situation of the entrance into the first pyramid, and plainly saw, that it was not in the centre of the pyramid. I observed that the passage ran in a straight line from the outside of the pyramid to the east side of the king's chamber; and this chamber being nearly in the centre of the pyramid, the entrance consequently must be as far from the middle of the

face as the distance from the centre of the chamber to the east side of it.

Having made this clear and simple observation, I found, that, if there were any chamber at all in the second pyramid, the entrance or passage could not be on the spot where I had excavated, which was in the centre, but calculating by the passage in the first pyramid, the entrance into the second would be near thirty feet to the east.

Satisfied with this calculation, I repaired to the second pyramid to examine the mass of rubbish. There I was not a little astonished when I perceived the same marks, which I had seen on the other spot in the centre, about thirty feet distant from where I stood. This gave me no little delight, and hope returned to cherish my pyramidical brains. I observed in this spot also, that the stones and mortar were not so compact as on the east side, which mark had given me so much encouragement to proceed in the first attempt; but what increased my hopes was an observation I made on the exterior of the front where the forced passage is. I observed the stones had been removed several feet from the surface of the pyramid, which I ascertained by drawing a line with the coating above to the basis below, and found the concavity was inclined to be deeper towards the spot where I intended to make my new attempt. Any traveller, who shall hereafter visit the pyramids, may plainly perceive this concavity above the true entrance. Such has been the effect of two different hints; first my old guide from Thebes, I mean the spots where the stony matter is not so compact as the surrounding mass; and, secondly, the concavity of the pyramid over the place where the entrance might have been expected to be found, according to the distance of the entrance into the first pyramid from its centre.

I immediately summoned the Arabs to work the next day. They were pleased at my recommencing the task, not in hopes of finding the entrance into the pyramid, but for the continuation of the pay they of course were to receive. As to expectation that the entrance might be found, they had none; and I often heard them utter, in a low voice, the word "*magnoon*," in plain English, madman. I pointed out to the Arabs the spot where they had to dig, and such was my measurement, that I was right within two feet, in a straight direction, as to the entrance into the first passage […]; and I have the pleasure of reckoning this day as fortunate, being that on which I discovered the entrance into the great tomb of Psammethis at Thebes. The Arabs began their work, and the rubbish proved to be as hard as that of the first excavation, with this addition, that we found larger blocks of stone in our way, which had belonged to the pyramid, besides the falling of the coating. The stones increased in size as we went on.

A few days after the visit of the Abbé de Forbin I was surprised by the appearance of another European traveller. It was the Chevalier Frediani, who, on his return from the second cataract of the Nile, came to visit the great pyramids. I had known him at Thebes on his ascending the Nile, and was much pleased to see him, as I thought he might be an impartial spectator of the event of my operations, which in fact he was. He greatly approved of my undertaking, but after being two days with me was ready to take his departure. I suppose he had as much expectation, that I should open the pyramid, as the Arabs who named me the *magnoon*. It happened, that on the very day he was to set off for Cairo, I perceived in the excavation a large block of granite, inclining downward at the same angle as the passage into the first pyramid, and pointing towards the centre. I requested the Chevalier to stay till the morrow, thinking perhaps he might have the pleasure of being one of the first who saw the entrance into the pyramid. He consented, and I was pleased to have a countryman of my own to be a witness of what passed on this important occasion. The discovery of the first granite stone occurred on the 28th of February, and on the 1st of March we uncovered three large blocks of granite, two on each side, and one on the top, all in an inclined direction towards the centre. My expectation and hope increased, as to all appearance, this must prove to be the object of my search. I was not mistaken, for on the next day, the 2nd of March, at noon, we came at last to the right entrance into the pyramid. The Arabs, whose expectation had also increased at the appearance of the three stones, were delighted at having found something new to show to the visitors, and get bakshis from them. Having cleared the front of the three stones, the entrance proved to be a passage four feet high, three feet six inches wide, formed of large blocks of granite, which descended towards the centre for a hundred and four feet five inches at an angle of twenty-six degrees. Nearly all this passage was filled up with large stones, which had fallen from the upper part, and as the passage is inclined downwards, they slid on till some larger than the rest stopped the way.

I had much ado to have all the stones drawn out of the passage, which was filled up to the entrance of the chamber. It took the remainder of this day and part of the next to clear it, and at last we reached a portcullis. At first sight it appeared to be a fixed block of stone, which stared me in the face, and said *ne plus ultra*, putting an end to all my projects as I thought; for it made a close joint with the groove at each side, and on the top it seemed as firm as those which formed the passage itself. On a close inspection however I perceived, that, at the bottom, it was raised about eight inches from the lower part of the groove, which is cut beneath to receive it; and I found, by this circumstance, that the large block before me was no more than a portcullis of granite, one foot three inches thick.

Having observed a small aperture at the upper part of the portcullis, I thrust a long piece of barley straw into it, and it entered upwards of three feet, which convinced me, that there was a vacuum ready to receive the portcullis. The raising of it was a work of no small consideration. The passage is only four feet high, and three feet six inches wide. When two men are in it abreast of each other they cannot move, and it required several men to raise a piece of granite not less than six feet high, five feet wide, and one foot three inches thick. The

levers could not be very long, otherwise there was not space in the four feet height to work with them; and if they were short, I could not employ men enough to raise the portcullis. The only method to be taken was, to raise it a little at a time; and by putting some stones in the grooves on each side, to support the portcullis while changing the fulcrum of the levers, it was raised high enough for a man to pass. An Arab then entered with a candle, and returned saying, that the place within was very fine. I continued to raise the portcullis, and at last made the entrance large enough to squeeze myself in; and after thirty days' exertion I had the pleasure of finding myself in the way to the central chamber of one of the two great pyramids of Egypt, which have long been the admiration of beholders. The Chevalier Frediani followed me, and after passing under the portcullis we entered a passage not higher or wider than the first. It was twenty-two feet seven inches long, and the works including the portcullis occupy six feet eleven inches in all. Where the granite work finishes at the end of this passage, there is a perpendicular shaft of fifteen feet, and at each side of the passage, and excavation in the solid rock, one of which, on the right as you enter, runs thirty feet in an upward direction, approaching the end of the lower part of the forced passage. [...] Before us we had a long passage running in a horizontal direction toward the centre. We descended the shaft by means of a rope. At the bottom of it I perceived another passage running downward at the same angle of 26° as that above, and toward the north. As my first object was the centre of the pyramid, I advanced that way, and ascended an inclined passage, which brought me to a horizontal one, that led toward the centre. I observed, that after we entered within the portcullis, the passages were all cut out of the solid rock. The passage leading toward the centre is five feet eleven inches high, and three feet six inches wide.

As we advanced farther on we found the sides of this passage covered with arborizations of nitre; some projecting in ropes, some not unlike the skin of a white lamb, and others so long as to resemble an endive-leaf. I reached the door at the centre of a large chamber. [...] I walked slowly two or three paces, and then stood still to contemplate the place where I was. Whatever it might be, I certainly considered myself in the centre of that pyramid, which from time immemorial had been the subject of the obscure conjectures of many hundred travellers, both ancient and modern. My torch, formed of a few wax candles, gave but a faint light; I could, however, clearly distinguish the principal objects. I naturally turned my eyes to the west end of the chamber, looking for the sarcophagus, which I strongly expected to see in the same situation as that in the first pyramid; but I was disappointed when I saw nothing there. The chamber has a painted ceiling; and many of the stones had been removed from their places, evidently by some one in search of treasure. On my advancing toward the west end, I was agreeably surprised to find, that there was a sarcophagus buried on a level with the floor.

By this time the Chevalier Frediani had entered also; and we took a general survey of the chamber, which I found to be forty-six feet three inches long, sixteen feet three inches wide, and twenty-three feet six inches high. It is cut out of the solid rock from the floor

to the roof, which is composed of large blocks of calcareous stone, meeting in the centre, and forming a roof of the same slope as the pyramid itself. The sarcophagus is eight feet long, three feet six inches wide, and two feet three inches deep in the inside. It is surrounded by large blocks of granite, apparently to prevent its removal, which could not be effected without great labour. The lid had been broken at the side, so that the sarcophagus was half open. It is of the finest granite; but, like the other in the first pyramid, there is not one hieroglyphic on it.

Looking at the inside, I perceived a great quantity of earth and stones, but did not observe the bones among the rubbish till the next day, as my attention was principally bent in search of some inscription that would throw light on the subject of this pyramid. We examined every part of the walls, and observed many scrawls executed with charcoal, but in unknown characters, and nearly imperceptible. They rubbed off into the dust at the slightest touch; and on the wall at the west end of the chamber I perceived an inscription in Arabic, as follows:

وفتحهم المعلم محمد احمد اجبار وذلك المعلم

عثمان حضر والملك علي محمد اولاً ولغلاك

and the various interpretations given of it compel me to explain some points, which will perhaps lead to a satisfactory explanation. It appears to me, that all the difficulty lies in the last letters of the inscription, which are supposed to be obscure. This indeed is the fact; but I must say, that these letters were so blotted on the wall, that they were scarcely visible. The transcriber was a Copt, whom I had brought from Cairo for the purpose, as I would not trust to my own pen; and not being satisfied of his protestations of accuracy, though it was copied under my own eyes, I invited many other persons, who were considered as the best skilled in the Arabic language of any in Cairo, and requested them to compare the copy with the original on the wall. They found it perfectly correct, except the concluding word, which indeed appeared obscure; but if it be considered how much that word resembles the right one, we shall find a correct sense, and the whole inscription made out.

Translation of the Inscription by
Mr. Salame.

"The Master Mohammed Ahmed lapicide, has opened them; and the Master Othman attended this (*opening*); and the King Alij Mohammed at first (*from the beginning*) to the closing up."

G. Belzoni, *Narrative of the Operations and Recent Discoveries within the Pyramids, Temples, Tombs, and Excavations, in Egypt and Nubia…*, London: John Murray, 1820

Khufu's Chamber

*At the 9th International Egyptologists' Congress, held
at Grenoble in September 2004, the architect Gilles
Dormion and his associate Jean-Yves Verd'hurt
announced that they had located a hitherto undiscovered
chamber at the heart of the Great Pyramid – news that
provoked a heated debate among Egyptologists. In an
interview given in early 2005, Jean-Pierre Corteggiani –
who, for his part, is convinced of the existence of the
hypothetical chamber – explains why the theory is more
than just speculation.*

*A few months ago, two amateur
Egyptologists announced that they had
located a new chamber in Khufu's
pyramid. The media reaction was scathing
and there was a huge scientific debate.
Do you think it's possible to find an
unopened burial chamber? Or should we
be sceptical? Is this just another instance
of Egyptomania?*

[I'm] glad to have a chance to answer
that. I'll try to make it simple and stick
to the main points.

I should start by saying that Gilles
Dormion and his associate Jean-Yves
Verd'hurt, the person he wrote the book
with – I know that for a fact because
they sent it to me chapter by chapter as
they went along – are not Egyptologists,
and have never claimed to be, but
they're certainly not 'amateurs' either.
Particularly not in the pejorative sense.
The way it seems to be understood by
people apparently so put out by their
discovery – if it is a discovery. [...]

They've approached this as architects.
And if being an Egyptologist means

being able to read hieroglyphs, you don't
need to be an Egyptologist to study a
monument, however mythical, that
doesn't have a single hieroglyphic
inscription! By the same token, you
don't have to be an architect to read
a well-written book that shows firstly
how well its authors know all the 4th-
dynasty pyramids, starting with the one
at Meidum. Their discovery of 'relieving
chambers' there showed how serious
their investigations were.

In the words of an Egyptologist and
architect friend of mine – because it's
exactly what I think – I'd describe
Dormion's book, *La Chambre de Chéops*,
as 'limpid and definitive' and even
'stunning'. Some people might perhaps
say that was excessive, but if one's going
to be excessive, I'd rather it was positive
than negative!

Despite things that have been said to
belittle it, the book makes no mention
of a 'secret chamber': it's careful to
speak of a 'presumed' or 'hypothetical'
chamber. And in arguing the case for
such a chamber, there's no suggestion

whatsoever that Khufu's mummy must be hidden somewhere in the monument because it hasn't been found! That would be tantamount to saying that every pharaoh whose body is missing must be secreted somewhere in the midst of his burial goods or – in media speak – his 'treasure'! Egyptologists (the bona fide ones) would really have their work cut out then!

Dormion and Verd'hurt start from a completely different observation. And when you read what they have to say you can't help wishing you'd made it yourself. All we have to do is note what's in front of our eyes. The 'King's Chamber' was clearly meant to be Khufu's burial chamber. But when the five 'relieving chambers' were built – which amounted to piling almost 2,500 tons of granite on top of limestone ashlar that was less dense – it caused a serious structural problem in this part of the pyramid. So it looks as if a decision was taken to re-use a funerary apartment that had been blocked up when plans changed during construction work.

It's worth remembering that, of all the pyramids, Khufu's has the most complex internal layout, and that there are in fact three 'chambers': the first, which was never finished, hollowed out of the bedrock about 30 metres down; the second, known as the 'Queen's Chamber', which is reached via the 'horizontal passage', and the 'King's Chamber', at the top of the very impressive 'Grand Gallery'. Some people – R. Stadelmann, for instance – think that this was a single project and that a 'three chamber system' was common to all pyramids, but it's evident from a number of important modifications that the project actually evolved over time. The 'Ascending Passage', for example, was cut out of existing courses of masonry, and the

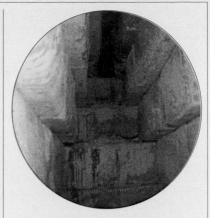

The architects Gilles Dormion and Jean-Yves Verd'hurt reached a number of conclusions about the Meidum pyramid which led to the discovery of two new chambers in 1998. Above: View of one of the chambers using an endoscope.

'well' had to be constructed as an exit route after the monument had been sealed.

When you are in the 'King's Chamber', all the way along the south wall there are obvious cracks on the underside of each of the nine ceiling beams, more or less where the beams meet. It's clear that there's been a serious 'accident', apparently due to the ashlar becoming compressed towards the south side of the chamber. There's evidence that the beams were firmly supported at both their northern and southern ends, probably using really big timbers cut from cedars of Lebanon. (There were no trees growing in Egypt that could have supplied timber supports that were almost 6 metres tall). But when you are underneath them, they only appear to be cracked at their southern end. So the people who were trying to stop the beams collapsing knew that they were cracked above as well, at their northern end, and they must have climbed up into the first 'relieving chamber' to check. This is crucial to Dormion's argument. Apart from the pyramid builders who could have known that there was a cavity above the 'King's Chamber'? And who would have been in a better position to know the exact level of the cavity and how to access it – which meant digging first in an easterly and not a southerly direction, as anybody looting the tomb would have done? What's more, any bounty hunters would have done exactly what Vyse and Perring did in 1837: on finding that the chamber had the same kind of roof structure as the 'King's Chamber', they would have tried to see if there was another chamber above and so broken into the four other 'relieving chambers'. So, in 1765, Davison didn't find the relieving chamber that's named after him, but only – and it's an important distinction – the ancient access to the inspection shaft excavated in the Grand

Gallery's uppermost corbel by the builders themselves! The Englishman was the first to enter the chamber in modern times, but it's apparent from contemporary travel accounts that people already knew that the chamber existed.

If what we've said so far is correct, it's logical to suppose that the Egyptians might have decided it would be better to bury Khufu somewhere else – given the extensive measures they took to prevent the chamber roof collapsing altogether. At the end of the 19th century, Flinders Petrie still thought this was ultimately inevitable, because of earth tremors. After Khufu's reign, no more chambers were ever located in the superstructure of a pyramid – proof that the architects of the time were pretty unnerved by the accident!

A glance at a cross-section of the pyramid shows that, with the subterranean chamber unfinished, the only possible choice, if there was one, had to be somewhere near the 'Queen's Chamber' and had to connect with it.

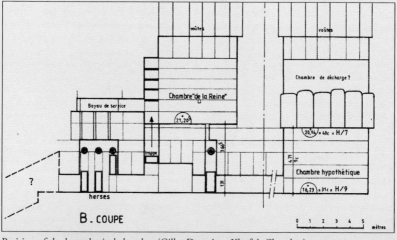

Position of the hypothetical chamber (Gilles Dormion, Khufu's Chamber)

There were various factors that led Dormion and Verd'hurt to conclude that the 'Queen's Chamber' was an operational area and that 'something had happened' here. There were some strange anomalies in the 'horizontal passage', for instance, and there was that curious niche with its access shaft, extended by a sap made by looters, and its unusual position in the east wall of the chamber, the absence of a permanent paved floor, and evidence of modifications to the under-paving. Dormion and Verd'hurt were collaborating closely at the time with the Supreme Council of Antiquities: not bad for amateurs who've got such a bad reputation now! They requested permission to use georadar – which was immediately granted – and set about verifying their theory, which was that the 'Queen's Chamber' gave access to an undiscovered area forming part of the second construction project (and not to a fourth funerary apartment excavated at a later date, as they have been stupidly misquoted as saying). Jean-Pierre Baron, a geophysicist with SAFEGE, came to take the necessary measurements on the floor of the chamber and completed a grid made up of 11 sets of readings taken on an east–west axis and 11 sets on a north–south axis. Baron was working in the dark, as he explained to me, because Dormion and Verd'hurt had deliberately not told him what they hoped to find. From the second passage onwards, he noticed that his radar registered a significant echo that was repeated ten times. This is what he says in his report:

'Analysis of the measurements taken on the floor of the chamber would seem to indicate the presence of a structure approximately a metre wide, orientated in an east–west direction, whose roof is about 3.5 metres below floor level. Its axis appears to be 2.5 metres out from the south wall of the chamber and to intersect it.'

What more can we say, except that what Baron is describing, absolutely exactly, is a passage two Egyptian cubits wide? That this passage is located on the pyramid's east–west axis? That logic tells us it must lead somewhere, and that this 'somewhere' is right in the heart of the pyramid, at the precise intersection of the east–west and north–south axes? That it seems to involve two or more, probably three portcullises? And that, in order to confirm its existence, all we need to do is to drill holes at two specially selected locations, insert optical fibres and backfill the holes with plaster?

Do you see where all this is heading? There's a fabulous amount at stake, so let's hope we get some answers soon!

I'd just like to add something I've said many times before: that SAFEGE was involved in helping to lay the TGV [French high-speed rail] network. When its engineers confirm that the ground is safe and they give the go-ahead for tracks to be built so that trains stuffed with passengers can travel at 300 kilometres an hour, it's just as well if they know what they're talking about! Why would one of them get it wrong when he comes to take georadar measurements in the Great Pyramid?

Jean-Pierre Corteggiani,
*Fous d'Égypte: Entretiens
avec Florence Quentin*,
Paris: Bayard, 2005

CHRONOLOGY OF THE PYRAMIDS

All of the kings from the 3rd to the 6th dynasties (2649–2150 BC) and a large number from the Middle Kingdom (essentially up until the 12th dynasty) were buried in pyramids. However, the symbolic burial sites of Khufu, Khafre and Menkaure are the largest and most perfect examples of the numerous pyramids that exist. From the famous step pyramid of Djoser at Saqqara, and the inscribed 'text' pyramids of the 6th-dynasty pharaohs and their wives, to the mudbrick constructions of their 12th-dynasty counterparts, one can trace the evolution of the pyramid over the course of a millennium.

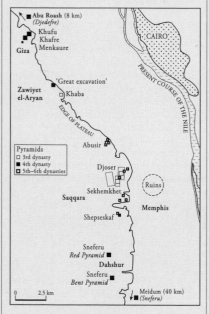

The names of the kings are followed by the name of the sites where their pyramids were built.

3rd dynasty (2649–2575 BC)
DJOSER: North Saqqara (step pyramid)
SEKHEMKHET: North Saqqara (unfinished pyramid)
KHABA: Zawiyet el-Aryan (step pyramid)
HUNI: Meidum (step pyramid)

4th dynasty (2575–2465 BC)
SNEFERU: Dahshur (Bent Pyramid and Red Pyramid); Meidum (built for Huni and transformed into a true pyramid by Sneferu)
KHUFU (CHEOPS): Giza (first Great Pyramid)
DJEDEFRE: Abu Roash
KHAFRE (CHEPHREN): Giza (second Great Pyramid)
MENKAURE (MYCERINUS): Giza (third Great Pyramid)
SHEPSESKAF: South Saqqara (Mastabat el-Fara'un)

5th dynasty (2465–2323 BC)
USERKAF: North Saqqara
SAHURE: Abusir
NEFERIRKARE: Abusir
RANEFEREF: Abusir
NIUSERRE: Abusir
DJEDKARE-ISESI: South Saqqara
UNAS: North Saqqara

6th dynasty (2323–2150 BC)
TETI: North Saqqara
PEPI I: North Saqqara
MERENRE: North Saqqara
PEPI II: North Saqqara

12th dynasty (1991–1783 BC)
AMENEMHET I: Lisht
SENWOSRET I (SESOSTRIS I): Lisht
AMENEMHET II: Dahshur
SENWOSRET II (SESOSTRIS II): al-Lahun
SENWOSRET III (SESOSTRIS III): Dahshur
AMENEMHET III: Dahshur and Hawara
AMENEMHET IV: Mazghuna

13th dynasty (1783–1640 BC)
KHENDJER: South Saqqara

BIBLIOGRAPHY

Archaeology
– Dormion, Gilles, *La Pyramide de Chéops. Architecture des appartements funéraires,* G. Dormion and J.-Y. Verd'hurt, Lyon, 1996; *La Chambre de Chéops,* Paris: Fayard, 2004
– Edwards, Iorwerth Eiddon Stephen, *The Pyramids of Egypt,* Harmondsworth: Penguin, 1975
– Fakhry, Ahmed, *The Pyramids,* Chicago: University of Chicago Press, 1961
– Goyon, Georges, *Les Inscriptions et Graffiti des voyageurs sur la Grande Pyramide,* Royal Geographical Society of Egypt, Cairo, 1944; *Le Secret des bâtisseurs des Grandes Pyramides, Khéops,* Paris: Pygmalion, 1977

– Hassan, Selim, *Excavations at Giza*, 10 vols,
Cairo: Oxford University Press/Egyptian Antiquities
Service, 1932–53
– Hawass, Zahi (ed.), *Trésors des pyramides*,
taken from *Reader's Digest*, Bagneux, 2003
– Jenkins, Nancy, *The Boat Beneath the Pyramid.
King Cheops' Royal Ship*, London: Thames &
Hudson, 1980
– Junker, Hermann, *Giza: Grabungen auf dem
Friedhof des Alten Reiches*, 12 vols, Vienna,
1929–55
– Lauer, Jean-Philippe, *Le Mystère des Pyramides*,
Paris: Presses de la Cité, 1988
– Lehner, Mark, *The Complete Pyramids*,
London: Thames & Hudson, 1997
– Maragioglio, Vito, and Rinaldi, Celeste,
L'Architettura delle Piramidi Menfite, vols IV, V, VI,
Rapallo: Officine Grafiche Canessa, 1965–67
– Nour, Mohammad Zaki, Osman, Mohamed Saleh,
Iskander, Zaky, and Mustafa, Ahmed Youssef,
The Cheops Boats, vol. I, Cairo: Government
Printing Office, 1960
– Perring, John S., *The Pyramids of Gizeh, from
actual survey and admeasurement*, I. *The Great
Pyramid*, II. *The Second and Third Pyramids…*,
III. *The Pyramids to the Southward of Gizeh and
at Abou Roash…*, London: James Fraser, 1839–42
– Petrie, William Matthew Flinders,
The Pyramids and Temples of Gizeh, London:
Field & Tuer-Simpkin, Marshall & Co., 1883
– Reisner, George, *Mycerinus: The Temples of
the Third Pyramid at Giza*, Cambrige (Mass.):
Harvard University Press, 1931; *A History of
the Giza Necropolis*, 2 vols (II. *The Tomb of
Hetepheres the Mother of Cheops*), Cambridge
(Mass.): Harvard University Press, 1955
– Stadelmann, Rainer, *Die ägyptischen Pyramiden.
Vom Ziegelbau zum Weltwunder*, Mainz: Philipp von
Zabern, 1985
– Tompkins, Peter, *Secrets of the Great Pyramid*,
New York: Harper & Row, 1971
– Verner, Miroslav, *The Pyramids: The Mystery,
Culture and Science of Egypt's Great Monuments*,
Cairo: AUC Press, 2000
– Vyse, Howard, *Operations Carried on at the
Pyramids of Gizeh in 1837*, 2 vols, London:
James Fraser, 1840–42
– Zivie-Coche, Christiane, *Sphinx: History of a
Monument*, translated by David Lorton, Ithaca (NY)
and London: Cornell University Press, 2002

– Bauval, Robert, and Gilbert, Adrian, *The Orion
Mystery: Unlocking the Secrets of the Pyramids*,
London: Heinemann, 1994
– Bauval, Robert, and Hancock, Graham,
*Keeper of Genesis: A Quest for the Hidden Legacy
of Mankind*, London: Heinemann, 1996
– Bertho, Joël, *La Pyramide reconstituée*,
Saint-Gely-du-Fesc: Éditions Unic, 2003
– Crozat, Pierre, *Le Génie des Pyramides*,
Paris: Dervy, 2002
– Davidovits, Joseph, *Ils ont bâti les pyramides*,
Paris: Jean-Cyrille Godefroy, 2002; *La Nouvelle
Histoire des Pyramides*, Paris: Jean-Cyrille Godefroy,
2004
– Davidson, David, and Aldersmith, Herbert,
The Great Pyramid, Its Divine Message, London:
The Covenant Publishing Company, 1961
– Houdin, Jean-Pierre and Henri, *La Pyramide de
Chéops, sa construction intégralement expliquée*,
Paris: Éditions du Linteau, 2003
– Jacobs, Edgar P., *Les Aventures de Blake et Mortimer:
Le Mystère de la Grande Pyramide*, Paris: Dargaud,
2005
– Lehner, Mark, *The Egyptian Heritage, based
on the Edgar Cayce Readings*, Virginia Beach:
A.R.E. Press, 1974
– Lewis, Harvey Spencer, *The Symbolic Prophecy of
the Great Pyramid*, San Jose: AMORC, 1936
– Pochan, André, *L'Énigme de la Grande Pyramide*,
Paris: Laffont, 1975
– Proctor, Richard, *The Great Pyramid: Observatory,
Tomb and Temple*, London: Chatto & Windus, 1883
– Taylor, John, *The Great Pyramid: Why Was
It Built? and Who Built It?*, London: Longman,
Green, Longman and Roberts, 1859

Theory and Fantasy

– Barbarin, Georges, *Le Secret de la Grande Pyramide
ou La Fin du monde adamique*, Paris: Adyar, 1951;
L'Énigme du Grand Sphinx, Paris: Adyar, 1974

LIST OF ILLUSTRATIONS

The following abbreviations have been used:
a above; *b* below; *c* centre; *l* left; *r* right

COVER

Front Aerial view of the pyramids of Khafre and Khufu.
Spine Detail of a triad representing Menkaure with the goddesses Hathor and Bat, 4th dynasty, sandstone statue. Egyptian Museum, Cairo.
Back View of the Sphinx and the Great Pyramid, watercolour by Louis-François Cassas, 1790.

OPENING

1 The pyramids and the Nile in flood.
2–3 View of the pyramids at the start of the 20th century.
4 Entrance to the Great Pyramid, photograph by Félix Bonfils, *c.* 1877. Musée des Monuments Français, Paris.
5 Tourists climbing the Great Pyramid, photograph by Félix Bonfils, 1875.
6–7 The Sphinx and the Great Pyramid, *c.* 1930.
9 The pyramid of Khafre with the tomb of Menkaure in the foreground.

CHAPTER 1

10 The Nile and the pyramids, detail from *Civitatis Orbis Terrarum* by Georg Braun and Franz Hogenberg, 1572. Private collection.
11al The Sphinx, engraving from André Thevet, *Cosmographie du Levant*, 1556. Bibliothèque Nationale de France [BnF], Paris.
11ar The Sphinx, engraving from Johann Helffrich, *Kurzer und warhafftiger Bericht von der Reis aus Venedig nach Hierusalem…*, 1579. Private collection.
11bl The Sphinx, engraving from *Les Voyages et observations du sieur La Boullaye-le-Gouz*, 1653. BnF, Paris.
11br The Sphinx, engraving from Frédéric-Louis Norden, *Voyage d'Égypte et de Nubie*, 1751. Private collection.
12a The word 'pyramid' in the tomb of Inherkhau, Luxor.
12–13b View of the three pyramids of Giza.
13r Representation of the Sphinx and pyramid on the stela of the scribe Montuher, 19th dynasty. Egyptian Museum, Cairo.

14 The Pyramid Texts in the antechamber of the pyramid of Unas, Saqqara, late 5th dynasty.
15 The building of the pyramids, coloured engraving, early 19th century.
16–17 *The Pyramids of Egypt*, engraving from a series on the Seven Wonders of the World by Maerten van Heemskerck, 16th century.
18 The pyramid of Caius Cestius, Rome, late 1st century BC.
19 Detail from *Scenes from the Life of Joseph*, mosaic, 13th century, dome of the basilica of St Mark, Venice.
20 and 21b Unidentified pyramids from an Arabic manuscript by Abu Hamid al-Gharnati, 16th-century copy of a 12th-century original. BnF, Paris.
21a Man on a camel, 12th-century drawing, Egypt. Louvre, Paris.
22 Map of the Nile and Cairo, from *The Book of Navigation* (*Kitâb-i bahriye*) by Piri Reis, Turkish manuscript, 16th century. BnF, Paris.
23 Rubbing of graffiti left by travellers at the entrance to the Great Pyramid.
24 The Pyramids of Egypt, miniature from *The Travels of Sir John Mandeville*, French manuscript, *c.* 1410–12. BnF, Paris.
25 The Pyramids of Egypt, engraving in Dapper, *Description de l'Afrique*, 1686. Private collection.
26a Title page from *Pyramidographia, or a Description of Pyramids in Ægypt* by John Greaves, 1646. Private collection.
26b (a) Father Vansleb, *Nouvelle relation en forme de journal d'un voyage fait en Égypte*, 1677. Private collection. (c) Benoît de Maillet, *Description de l'Égypte*, 1735. Private collection. (b) Frédéric-Louis Norden, *Voyage d'Égypte et de Nubie*, 1765 edition. Private collection.
27 Plan of the interior of the Great Pyramid, engraving from Benoît de Maillet, *Description de l'Égypte*, 1735. Private collection.

CHAPTER 2

28 *Bonaparte Rallies his Armies before the Battle of the Pyramids, 21 July 1798* (detail), painting by Baron Gros. Châteaux de Versailles and Trianon.
29 Title page of *Description de l'Égypte*, published on the orders of Napoleon, volume I, 1809.
30 *Expedition to Egypt on the Orders of Bonaparte*, detail of the ceiling of the Campana room by Léon Cogniet (1794–1880). Louvre, Paris.

31l Cross-section of the portcullis chamber, between the Grand Gallery and the king's chamber, engraving from *Description de l'Égypte*, volume V, 1822.

31r Views of the Grand Gallery in the Great Pyramid, seen from the upper level and the lower level, engraving, idem.

32–33a Topographical plan of the pyramids of Memphis, engraving, idem.

32–33b *The Pyramids of Memphis*, also known as *View of the Pyramids and the Sphinx at Sunset*, watercolour by Charles Balzac (1752–1820). Louvre, Paris.

34 Chamber and sarcophagus in the Great Pyramid, engraving from Luigi Mayer, *Views in Egypt*, 1804.

35 Moving between the second and the third gallery in the Great Pyramid, idem.

36al and 36ar Entrance and cross-section of the pyramid of Khafre, engravings from Giovanni Belzoni, *Travels in Egypt and Nubia*, 1821.

36b Portrait of Giovanni Belzoni, engraving, c. 1820. Bibliothèque des Arts Décoratifs, Paris.

37al Entrance to the funerary chamber of the pyramid of Khafre, engraving from Giovanni Belzoni, *Travels in Egypt and Nubia*, 1821.

37ar Inscription by Belzoni on the wall of the funerary chamber of the pyramid of Khafre.

38a Portrait of Champollion, detail from *Members of the Franco-Tuscan Expedition to Egypt in 1828–29*, painting by G. Angelleli. Museo Archeologico, Florence.

38b Extract translated from the 'Note to the Viceroy on the Conservation of the Monuments of Egypt', from Champollion, *Lettres écrites d'Égypte et de Nubie en 1828 et 1829.*

39 Pyramid of Khafre stripped of most of its limestone casing, with the pyramid of Khufu in the foreground.

40 Relieving chambers above the king's chamber, engraving from Howard Vyse, *Operations Carried on at the Pyramids of Gizeh in 1837*, 1840–42.

41a Graffiti in the fifth relieving chamber, reputedly by Campbell.

41b Inscription and cartouche of Khufu in one of the relieving chambers.

42l Funerary chamber and sarcophagus in the third pyramid, engraving by John S. Perring from Howard Vyse, *Operations Carried on at the Pyramids of Gizeh in 1837*, 1840–42.

42r Fragments of the wooden coffin found in the pyramid of Menkaure, engraving, idem.

43 View of the third pyramid, engraving from John Perring, *The Pyramids of Gizeh*, 1839.

44 Title page of *Denkmaeler aus Aegypten und Aethiopien* by Karl Richard Lepsius, 1849–59.

45 *The Prussian Expedition to Egypt, Led by Lepsius, at the Summit of the Pyramid of Cheops at Giza*, watercolour by Johann Jakob Frey. Ägyptisches Museum und Papyrussammlung, Berlin.

CHAPTER 3

46 The valley temple of Khafre near the Sphinx after its clearance by Auguste Mariette, photograph by Richard Morris Hunt, c. 1870.

47 Portrait of George A. Reisner in Giza, March 1929. Harvard University, Boston Museum of Fine Arts Expedition.

48l Portrait of Khufu, 4th dynasty, diorite statue found in the valley temple of the pyramid. Egyptian Museum, Cairo.

48r Interior of the valley temple of Khafre.

49 Auguste Mariette at the entrance of the valley temple of Khafre, photograph. Bibliothèque de l'Institut de France, Maspero collection, Paris.

50 Papers of Auguste Mariette: frontal view of the Sphinx with the excavations in the foreground, watercolour, 1853. Ibidem.

51 Copy of an inscription on one of the statues of Khafre, handwritten by Auguste Mariette. Ibidem.

52a Measuring the entrance to the Great Pyramid, photograph by Charles Piazzi Smyth, 1865. National Museum of Photography, Film and Television, Bradford.

52b Portrait of William Matthew Flinders Petrie on one of his expeditions to Giza, 1880–82.

53 *Plan of the Triangulation of the Survey of 1881 around the Pyramids of Gizeh*, engraving from William Matthew Flinders Petrie, *The Pyramids and Temples of Gizeh*, 1883.

54 The Sphinx, photograph, c. 1870.

55 Portrait of Gaston Maspero in Karnak, 1900.

56l Excavation of the head of the colossal statue of Menkaure, Menkaure's mortuary temple, 14 April 1907. Harvard University, Boston Museum of Fine Arts Expedition.

56r Alabaster statue of Menkaure from mortuary temple, 4th dynasty. Museum of Fine Arts, Boston.

57 Discovery of the triads of Menkaure, valley temple, 11 July 1908. Harvard University, Boston Museum of Fine Arts Expedition.

58–59b Sarcophagus of Queen Hetepheres being raised from her tomb, 17 April 1927, eastern necropolis of Giza. Ibidem.

59a Noel F. Wheeler inside the tomb of Hetepheres, 22 July 1926.

60a Interior view of the tomb of Hetepheres, 1 October 1926. Ibidem.

60c Carrying chair from the tomb of Hetepheres, 4th dynasty, reign of Sneferu. Egyptian Museum, Cairo. Ibidem.

60–61b Gilded and inlaid curtain box, idem.

61a Remains of a jewelry chest excavated on 25 July 1926, idem. Harvard University, Boston Museum of Fine Arts Expedition.

61c Gilded box containing silver bracelets set with carnelian, lapis lazuli and turquoise, idem.

62a Discovery of the pit containing the boat of Khufu, still sealed with limestone slabs, 1954.

62b Inscription on one of the slabs that sealed the pit containing the boat of Khufu. It mentions the name of Djedefre, son of Khufu.

63a Reassembled boat of Khufu, 1960s.

63b Khufu's boat after its reassembly, cedarwood and acacia, 4th dynasty. Solar Barque Museum, Giza.

64 3D reconstruction of the Khafre pyramid complex seen from the south-east, created in 1998 as part of the Giza Plateau Mapping Project, directed by Mark Lehner. Oriental Institute, University of Chicago.

65 Remains of the satellite pyramid of Khufu.

CHAPTER 4

66 Pyramid of Khafre and Western Field cemetery.

67 Cross-section of the mastabas of Giza, computer graphic. Edigraphie, Rouen.

68 Pyramid of Menkaure and mortuary temple.

69 Aerial view of the pyramids, reconstruction by Jean-Claude Golvin.

70a Pyramids of the queens of Menkaure.

70b Sarcophagus decorated like a palace façade, painted limestone, 4th dynasty, from a mastaba east of the pyramid of Khufu. Egyptian Museum, Cairo.

71 Detail of the pyramid of Khufu showing one of the boat pits and the building that now houses the boat discovered in 1954, photograph, 1981.

72 Statues of the queen and her family, chapel of the mastaba of Queen Meresankh, 4th dynasty.

73l Bas-reliefs of the prince and his wife Nefretkau, chapel of the mastaba of Prince Khufukhaf, 4th dynasty.

73r Statuette of the priest Kay, painted limestone, 4th dynasty, from the western necropolis at Giza. Egyptian Museum, Cairo.

74a Aerial view of the pyramid of Khufu.

74b Statuette of Khufu, ivory, 4th dynasty, from Abydos. Egyptian Museum, Cairo.

75 Grand Gallery of the pyramid of Khufu.

76 Cross-section of the pyramid of Khufu, computer graphic. Edigraphie, Rouen.

77a Original entrance to the pyramid of Khufu and the breach made by al-Mamun, aerial photograph.

77b Junction of the al-Mamun breach with the Ascending Passage in the Great Pyramid.

78 Funerary complex of the pyramid of Khafre with the causeway leading to the valley temple and the Sphinx, aerial photograph.

79a Cross-section of the pyramid of Khafre, computer graphic. Edigraphie, Rouen.

79b Detail of the statue of Khafre protected by the god Horus, diorite, 4th dynasty. Egyptian Museum, Cairo.

80a Head of Menkaure (valley temple), alabaster, 4th dynasty. Museum of Fine Arts, Boston.

80b Antechamber of the pyramid of Menkaure, decorated like a palace façade.

81al Breach in the pyramid of Menkaure.

81ar Remains of the red granite casing on the base of the pyramid of Menkaure.

81r Cross-section of the pyramid of Menkaure, computer graphic. Edigraphie, Rouen.

82 Aerial view of the Sphinx.

83a Detail of the head of the Sphinx.

83b Detail of the restorations to the rear of the Sphinx.

CHAPTER 5

84 Illustration from *Aventures de Blake et Mortimer: Le Mystère de la Grande Pyramide* by the Belgian comic-book artist Edgar P. Jacobs, Éditions Dargaud-Lombard, 1986.

85l Cover of *La Pyramide Reconstituée* by Joël Bertho, Éditions Uniques, 2003.

85ar Cover of *The Egyptian Heritage based on the Edgar Cayce Readings* by Mark Lehner, ARE Press, Virginia Beach, 1974.

85br Cover of *The Symbolic Prophecy of the Great Pyramid* by H. Spencer Lewis, AMORC, San Jose, 1936.

86 Astronomers in the observatory of the pyramid of Khufu, engraving, *La Nature*, 11 April 1891.

87 Cross-section of the Great Pyramid of Giza, showing its positioning relative to the stars, postcard, early 20th century.

88 'Isometric projection showing entrance doorway of horizontal passage to Queen's Chamber', illustration from *The Great Pyramid, Its Divine Message* by David Davidson, 1924.

89al 'Placement of prophetic dates, after Davidson and Aldersmith', engraving from

Georges Barbarin, *L'Enigme du Grand Sphinx*, Adyar, Paris, 1949.
89al Covers of Georges Barbarin, *L'Enigme du Grand Sphinx*, Adyar, Paris, 1949 and *Le Secret de la Grande Pyramide*, Adyar, Paris, 1936.
89b Red granite sarcophagus in the funerary chamber of Khufu.
90a 'Lifting machines used in the construction of the pyramids', engraving illustrating the theory of Herodotus, *Technische Rundschau*, October 1952.
90b Different types of ramp that could have been used to transport blocks of stone.
91 Hypothetical interior ramp in the pyramid of Khufu, 3D model by Jean-Pierre Houdin.
92 Densities of the Great Pyramid, microgravimetric measurements carried out by the Fondation EDF, 1986–87.
93al and 93ar The Pyramid Rover robot being used to explore the Queen's Chamber, an experiment carried out with the support of the Egyptian Antiquities Council, *National Geographic* and the company iRobot in September 2002.
94a and 94b Georadar mapping of the floor of the Queen's Chamber, directed by Gilles Dormion with the support of SAFEGE, Autumn 2000.

95 Interior of the 'queen's chamber' and its niche.
96 The Giza plateau and the Pyramids, photograph from the satellite IKONOS, 6 December 1999.

DOCUMENTS

97 The Sphinx, engraving from Frédéric-Louis Norden, *Voyage d'Égypte et de Nubie*, 1751. Private collection.
117 Endoscopic view of one of the two relieving chambers of the pyramid of Meidum discovered by Gilles Dormion and Jean-Yves Verd'hurt in 1998.
118 Cross-section of the hypothesized chamber inside the pyramid of Khufu, from Gilles Dormion, *La Chambre de Chéops*, Fayard, Paris, 2004.
120 Map of the major pyramids of Egypt, computer graphic. Edigraphie, Rouen.
121 Travellers at the pyramids of Giza, from George Sandys, *Relation of a Journey Begun in 1610*. BnF, Paris.

INDEX

A – B

Abd al-Latif 20, 103–4
Aboukir, Battle of *29*
Abu Ghurob (site) 89
Abu Roash 12, *22*, 79, *79*
Alexander the Great 30
al-Gharnati, Abu Hamid (also known as al-Qaysi/al-Andalusi) 20–21, *20*
Ali, Muhammad 36, *38*, 39, 40
al-Mamun, Abdallah 21, *76*, 77, *77*
al-Maqrizi 19, 22
al-Masudi, Ali 21
Alpha Centauri (star) 87
Alpha Draconis (star) *52*, 87, *87*
al-Rashid, Haroun 21
Amenemhet I, pyramid of (Lisht) 75

Ammianus Marcellinus *12*, 18, 23
Anastasi, Giovanni 33
Antipater of Sidon 16
Aswan, red granite of 79, 81, *81*, 90

Balzac, Charles *32–33*
Barbarin, Georges 88, *88*
Baron, Jean-Pierre 94
Belzoni, Giovanni 36–37, *36*, *37*, 41, 111–15
Bertho, Joël 90
Blavatsky, Helena 88, *89*
Bonaparte, Napoleon 26, *29*, 30, *30*, *35*, 38, *71*
Borchardt, Ludwig 55, *69*, 76
Bouriant, Urbain 19

C

Cairo *11*, *20*, 21, *22*, 59
Caius Cestius, pyramid of (Rome) *18*, 24

Campbell (Consul) 40, 41, *41*
Cassius Dio 78
Caviglia, Giovanni Battista 36, 40, 41, 49
Cayce, Edgar 90
Champollion, Jean-François *35*, *36*, 37–38, *38*, 44
Charles the Bold 23
Chateaubriand, François René de 109–10
Constantine the Great 18
Corteggiani, Jean-Pierre 116–19
Coutelle, Jean-Marie 30–31, *30*, 36

D

Dahshur (site) 12, *61*
Dapper, Olfert *25*
Davidovits, Joseph 90
Davidson, David 87–88, *88*

Davison, Nathaniel *23*, 40–41
Delille, Abbé *23*
Denon, Dominique Vivant *35*, 109
Description de l'Égypte 29, 30–31, 32, *35*, 44
Diodororus Siculus 16, 89, 99–101
Dixon, Waynman *93*
Djedefre:
– Pharaoh *63*, 79
– pyramid of (Abu Roash) *22*
Djoser, pyramid of (Saqqara) 13, *64*
Dormion, Gilles 81, 91, 92–93, *118*
Dream Stela 24, 49, *55*
Drovetti, Bernardino 33

E – F – G – H

Egyptian Antiquities Organization 90–91

Egyptian expedition 29–33
Elephantine 48
Erman, Adolf 85, 86, 88

Fisher, Clarence 59
Fourmont, Claude Louis 26
Frederick William IV (King of Prussia) 44
French Institute of Oriental Archaeology, Cairo 89

Gabri, Ali 54
Gantenbrink, Rudolf 92
German Archaeological Institute, Cairo 92
Giza Plateau Mapping Project 65
Goidin, Jean-Patrice 91
Goyon, Georges 32
Greaves, John 25

Harant, Krystof 23, *24*
Hassan, Selim 58
Hawara (site) 55
Hawass, Zahi 64, 65, 92
Helena of Constantinople 19
Henutsen, Queen 49
Hermes (god) 22
Herodotus 14–15, *15*, 16, 74, 89, 91, 98–99
Hetepheres, tomb of Queen (Giza) *47*, 56, 58, *58*, *59*, 61
Hölscher, Uvo 79
Horemakhet (god) *13*
Horus (god) 13, 49
Houdin, Jean-Pierre and Henri 90, *91*
Huntington, Robert 24

I – J

Ibn Battuta 11, 12
Illahun (site) 55

Jacobs, Edgar P. *85*
Jean de Mandeville 24, *24*
Joint Egyptian Expedition of Harvard University and the Boston Museum of Fine Arts 55

Jomard, Edme-François 32, 87
Joseph's granaries 19, *19*, 23, 86
Junker, Hermann 58

K – L

Kawab, mastaba of *58*
Kay, statue of *73*
Kerisel, Jean 91–92
Khafre (Chephren):
– burial chamber 37, *37*;
– mortuary temple 70, *78*, 79;
– Pharaoh *48*, 49, *49*, 79, *79*;
– pyramid of 12, *12*, *15*, 20, *33*, 36–37, *37*, *39*, 40, 41, 55, 56, 59, *64*, 69, 79, *79*, 80, *90*, 94;
– valley temple 48, 49, *49*, 52, 57, 70, *78*, 79
Khufu (Cheops):
– boats *63*, 64, *65*, 70–71, *71*;
– breach of al-Mamun 76, 77, *77*;
– causeway *58*, *61*, 74–75;
– Grand Gallery 25, *30*, *31*, *35*, 75, 76, 77, *77*, 86, 87, 93;
– Great Pyramid 12, *12*, *15*, 20, 21, 23, *23*, 24, 25, 26, *27*, 31–33, *31*, 36–37, 38–39, 40–41, *40*, 44, *44*, 48, 52–54, *52*, *53*, 56, 59, *63*, 64, *71*, *73*, 74–78, *74*, 79, *79*, 80–81, 85, 86, *87*, *90*, 92–95, *92*;
– King's Chamber *30*, *40*, 41, 54, *89*, 92, 93;
– mortuary temple *58*, 64, 74;
– Pharaoh 24, 41, *41*, *47*, 56, *58*, *61*, *63*, *70*, *74*;
– Queen's Chamber 36, 76–77, *76*, 91, 92, *93*, 94, *94*, *95*;
– satellite pyramid 64, 70;

– 'stress-relieving chambers' *23*, *31*, 40, *40*, 77, 93, 94;
– Subterranean Chamber 25, *27*, 92, 94;
– valley temple *58*, 65, 75
Khufuankh, sarcophagus of 49
Khufukhaf, mastaba of Prince *73*
Kléber (General) 30

Lauer, Jean-Philippe *64*, 74
Lehner, Mark 65
Lepère, Jean-Baptiste 30, 32, 36
Lepsius, Karl Richard 29, 44, *44–45*
Lewis, Spencer 88
Linant de Bellefonds, Louis 39
Lisht (site) 75, 89
Luynes (Duc de) 48

M – N

Maillet, Benoît de 26, *27*
Mandeville, (Sir) John 23, *24*
Mariette, Auguste 47, *47*, 48–49, *49*, 55, 57, 68, 79
Maspero, Gaston 55, *55*
Mayer, Luigi *35*
Meidum:
– pyramid of 12, 55, 77, 89;
– 'relieving chambers' 94
Memphis (site) 18, 31, *33*
Menkaure (Mycerinus):
– burial chamber 42–43, *43*;
– mortuary temple 56, *56*;
– Pharaoh *15*, *56*, 57, *57*, 80–81, *80*;
– pyramid of 12, *12*, 18, 22, *33*, 39, 40, 41–43, 56, *65*, *68*, 70, *70*, 80–81, *92*;

– queens' pyramids *70*;
– valley temple 56, 57, *57*, *80*
Menou, (General) Jacques-François de 30
Mercator, Gerardus 23
Meresankh, mastaba of Queen *73*
Meroë, pyramids of (Sudan) *18*
Minguez, Manuel 90
Montuher, stela of the scribe 13, *13*
Morison, Anthoine 67, 68

Nakhla, Chawki 81
Nazlet el-Samman 65, 75
Necropolis (Giza) 53–54, 55–56, 58–59, 65, *67*, 68–71, *70*, *71*, *73*
Neferirkare, pyramid 69
Nelson (Lord) 41
Niuserre, pyramid of 69
Norden, Frederick 26
Nouet, Nicolas Antoine 32

P – Q

Perring, John 40, 41, *41*, 43, 56, *81*
Petrie, Flinders 22, *52*, 53, *53*, 54, 55, *74*
Philo of Byzantium 16
Piri Reis 22
Plato *12*
Pliny the Elder 18, 48, 101–2
Pochan, André 88
Pococke, Richard 26
Prisse d'Avennes, Émile *35*
Proctor, Richard *86*, 87
Pyramid Texts 14, *15*, *43*

Qin Shi Huang, mausoleum of 12

R – S

Ramesses II 13
Reisner, George *47*, 55, 56, 57, *57*
Rosellini, Ippolito *35*, 38

Rufinus of Aquileia 19
Rutherford, Adam 88

SAFEGE 94
Sahure, pyramid of *69*
Said Pasha 47
Saladin (Sultan) 21, *22*,
   42, 81
Salt, Henry 33
Sandys, George 105–6
Saqqara 12, 13, *15*, 43,
   44, 48, *64*
Savary, Claude 26
Schiaparelli, Ernesto
   55
Septimius Severus 18,
   78
Seti I 37
Seven Wonders of the
   World 15–16, *16*, *17*,
   18
Shepseskaf 57, 81

Sieglin, Ernst von 79
Sloan (Vice Consul)
   40
Smyth, Charles Piazzi 52,
   52, 53, 54, 86
Sneferu *61*
Sphinx *11*, 13, *13*,
   23–24, *25*, 31, *32*, *33*,
   36, 48, *49*, 52, *54*, 55,
   55, 58, 59, *83*
Stadelmann, Rainer 76
Steindorff, Georg 55
Strabo 16, 17–18, 54,
   77
Strub-Roessler, Hermann
   90
Sudan *18*, 24, 56
Supreme Council of
   Antiquities (Egypt) 64,
   73
Surid, legend of King
   22

T – U – V

Tanis 48
Taylor, John 52, 86
Theodosius I 19
Thévenot, Jean de 26
Thevet, André 24
Thutmose IV 24, *55*
Turah limestone
   15, 89

Unas, pyramid of
   (Saqqara) *15*

Valley of the Kings 37,
   70
Van der Aa, Pieter *25*
Van Ghistele, Joos 23
Van Heemskerck,
   Maerten *16–17*
Vansleb (Father) 26

Verd'hurt, Jean-Yves 81,
   92–93
Veryard, Ellis 25, 106–7
Volney, (Count)
   Constantin François de
   26, 107–8
Vyse, Colonel Howard
   40, *40*, 41–43, 54, 56,
   81

W

Waseda University 91
Wellington (Duke of) 41
Wheeler, Noel *59*

Y

Yoshimura, Sakuji 91
Youssef, Ahmed 64

PICTURE CREDITS

Altitude/Yann Arthus-Bertrand front cover, 77a, 82. Archives Gallimard 13r, 16–17, 26a, 29, 31l, 31r, 32–33a, 34, 36al, 37al, 38b, 40, 43, 55, 121. Archives White Star 15. Archives White Star/Araldo De Luca 14, 37ar, 61c, 62a, 63a, 72, 73l, 89b, 95. Archives White Star/Giulio Veggi 65, 70a. Archives White Star/Marcello Bertinetti 68, 78. Art Archive 36ar. Art Archive/Dagli-Orti /Archaeological Museum, Florence 38a. Art Archive/Dagli-Orti 80b. Art Archive/Dagli-Orti/Bibliothèque des Arts décoratifs, Paris 35, 36b. Art Archive/Dagli-Orti/Egyptian Museum, Cairo spine, 74b, 79b. Art Archive/Dagli-Orti/Solar Barque Museum, Giza 63b. BnF, Paris 20, 21b, 22, 24. BPK, Berlin, Dist RMN/Margarete Büsing 45. Bridgeman Art Library/Museum of Fine Arts, Boston 80a. Private collection 10, 11, 12a, 23, 26c(1), 26c (2), 26b, 27, 42l, 42r, 53, 62b, 85, 88, 89al, 89ar, 90a, 97. Stéphane Compoint 66, 75. Corbis/Bettmann 46. Corbis/Barnabas Bosshart 71. Corbis/Bill Ross 18. Corbis/Hulton-Deutsch Collection 6–7. Corbis/Larry Lee 9. Corbis/Webistan/Reza 74a. Corbis/Peter M. Wilson 12–13b. Corbis/Stapleton Collection back cover. Jean-Pierre Corteggiani 39, 41a, 41b, 48r, 77b, 81al, 81ar, 83a, 83b. Araldo De Luca 48l, 60c, 60–61b. All Rights Reserved. 90b. Gilles Dormion and Jean-Yves Verd'hurt 94a, 94b, 117, 118. EDF MTS 92. Gamma/Xavier Rossi 73r. Jean-Claude Golvin 69. Jean-Pierre Houdin 91. Keystone 2–3. Kharbine-Tapabor/Avant-Demain 5. Jürgen Liepe 70b. Mary Evans Picture Library 86, 87. © 2006 Museum of Fine Arts, Boston 56r. © 2006 Museum of Fine Arts, Boston/Mustapha Abu-el-Hamd 59a, 60a, 61a. © 2006 Museum of Fine Arts, Boston/Badawi Ahmed 57. © 2006 Museum of Fine Arts, Boston/Said Ahmed 56l. © 2006 Museum of Fine Arts, Boston/Mohammedani Ibrahim 47, 58–59b. National Museum of Photography, Film and Television, Bradford 52a. Oriental Institute, University of Chicago 64. Petrie Museum, University College, London 52b. RMN/Daniel Arnaudet 30. RMN/Daniel Arnaudet/Jean Schormans 28. RMN/Michèle Bellot 32–33b. RMN/Jean-Gilles Berizzi 4. RMN/Gérard Blot 49, 50, 51. RMN/Hervé Lewandoski 21a. Roger Viollet 54. Roger-Viollet/Lapi 1. Scala, Florence 19. Sipa/AP- Space Imaging 96. Sipa/AP-Stringer/Mohammad al Sehety 93al, 93ar. Jean Vigne 25. © 2006 Éditions Blake et Mortimer/Studio Jacobs n.v. Dargaud-Lombard s.a. 84.

ACKNOWLEDGMENTS

For reasons known to the individuals concerned, the author would like to thank the following people: above all Nadine Cherpion, but also Jean-Pierre Baron, Gilles Dormion, Jean-Yves Empereur, Victor Ghica, Denis Maraval, Gérard Roquet, Bruno Santerre, Michel Valloggia and Jean-Yves Verd'hurt, and last but not least Any-Claude, Marjorie and, of course, Élisabeth at Gallimard.

Egyptologist Jean-Pierre Corteggiani is in charge of scientific and technical relations
at the Institut Français d'Archéologie Orientale (IFAO), based in Cairo.
He is author or co-author of a number of publications about Egypt, including
The Egypt of the Pharaohs at the Cairo Museum (London: Scala, 1987).

For Natalie…

Translated from the French *Les Grandes Pyramides: Chronique d'un mythe* by Ruth Sharman

Library of Congress Control Number: 2007929682

ISBN 10: 0-8109-9458-5
ISBN 13: 978-0-8109-9458-4

Printed and bound in Italy
10 9 8 7 6 5 4 3 2 1

HNA ■■■■■
harry n. abrams, inc.
a subsidiary of La Martinière Groupe

115 West 18th Street   New York, NY 10011
www.hnabooks.com